Power Talk

With

PowerPoint

2010

Gerald D Kruse

ISBN: 0-9815098-5-1
ISBN-13: 978-0-9815098-5-3

DEDICATION

I would like to dedicate this book to the three people that make the biggest difference in my life; my Mom, my wife, and my son.

Without my Mom I would not have the chance to write and help others. She is and always has been there for me. I love you Mom.

My wife Anna has put up with me and let me have the freedom that I needed to goof off till I could decide what to do.

My son Brian has encouraged me to be better. And I write this book so that during his career he will not have to sit through boring executive's presentation like I did for many years of my professional career. Brian has edited all my books prior to this one and has giving me good advice on how to improve my writing skills. He has worked hard on his education and his career and it is my wish that he will be able to benefit from this book and that he will be able to give an exciting and entertaining presentation when he is asked. Giving boring and uninformative presentations can be a career killer. It has been said that the only thing worse than having to sit through a boring presentation is giving one. Brian, keep your career moving forward and always remember, a presentation should be informative and entertaining. It takes good story telling skills and good slides to get your point across.

Table of Contents

ACKNOWLEDGEMENTS

I would like to acknowledge those that helped with this book, especially to my students and audiences that asked me questions, which gave me ideas for this book.

Please visit my website: http://www.KrusePowerTalk.com

Disclaimer

Because this book is about a Microsoft product, I must tell you that not all the operations will operate exactly the same every time, nor will your changes you make to the PowerPoint presentation be stable. Microsoft products have been known to be unstable, yet very powerful. Many times you will find that the same process used over and over will get different results. No you are not going crazy, this is just the results of prioritizing profits before quality. This is the age in which we live. Microsoft has seemed to perfected this process even though they cannot produce a prefect product. It is sad, but this has seemed to be the state of affairs that our hi-tech world has chosen instead of building a quality product. And because we mere mortals that have to use their products in our everyday lives, have no control over the development of their products we have to work with the outcome of using their products. I also cannot be held responsible for the outcomes that you might have. I have tested the steps in this book and they work over 98% of the time on my computer. You may have different results. The information in this book is distributed on an "As Is" basis, without warranty. While every precaution has been taken in the preparation of the book, neither the author nor the publisher shall have any liability to any person or entity with respect to any loss or damage caused or alleged to be caused directly or indirectly by the instructions contained in this book or by the computer software and hardware described in it.

Trademarks and Registered names are used. Rather than put a trademark or registered symbol in every occurrence of a trademarked or registered name, we state we are using the names only in an editorial fashion and to benefit of the trademark and register owner with no intention of infringement of the trademark or register. No such use, or the use of any trade name is intended to convey endorsement or other affiliation with this book.

Chapter 1 Introduction

PowerPoint is the most popular presentation software. Some guess that over 30,000,000 people use PowerPoint daily. Most Windows computers have PowerPoint installed (and many Apple computers have PowerPoint for Mac), which means that a presentation can be saved on a disk or flash drive and be presented on almost any office computer. Many of the commands in PowerPoint are common to other Microsoft programs. The **Home** tab in PowerPoint is very similar to the commands found in Microsoft Word. Fonts, color, size, and other commands for text can be altered in PowerPoint the same way in which Word handles text. The ribbon used in PowerPoint 2007 has slightly been altered. If the ribbon is not visible click on the Expand/Minimize arrow next to the question mark in the upper right corner.

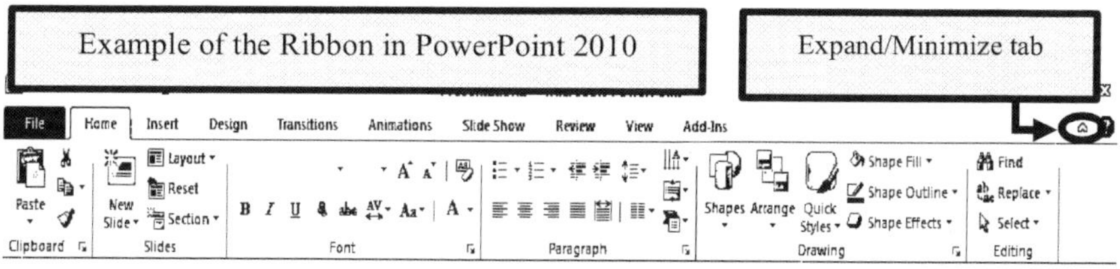

General Breakdown of Tabs:

PowerPoint will automatically open to a blank Title Page, with a placeholder for the title and a subtitle. When PowerPoint opens on a title page you can click anywhere inside the Text Box to start typing. If you desire a different layout, *click* on **File** and then *click* on the down arrow next to **New**, there are different templates and themes that can be selected. You can also *click* on the **File** tab and open an existing file or new presentations with templates. Under the **File** tab is also where you can add new ribbon tabs and add-ins. Also, under the **File – Options** tabs additional tabs can be added to the ribbon (**Custom Ribbon**) and additional tools can be added to the **Quick Access Toolbar**. The **File** tab is also where you print the presentation or save the presentation. You also have options for your presentation layout or the layout of PowerPoint.

The **Home** tab has commands for adjusting font type, color, and size. You can also arrange objects to overlap other objects, deciding on which object should be brought forward or sent backwards. Under the **Home** tab can be used to find and replace items. The **Home** tab is very similar to using Word commands.

The **Insert** tab is for inserting pictures, clip art, shapes, smart art, charts, equations, symbols, videos and audio.

The **Design** tab is where template layouts and page setup can be found, for changing the look of the presentation and adding a personal touch.

The **Transitions** tab has a variety of transitions that go in between slides during a slide show, making a smooth flow from one slide to another. Under the **Transition** tab sound can also be added to coordinate with the transitions.

Under the **Animations** tab are commands for moving text, pictures or even videos across the presentation while in a slide show.

The **Slide Show** tab has commands for setting up your slide show, setting timing for automating the slide show, add narrations to the slide show and the buttons to start the slide show.

Under the **Review** tab are commands for spell check, translation, language selection and buttons for checking over your work before you present it.

The **View** tab gives options for screen layout, setting up a master layout, adding ruler and gridlines to the page, viewing screen in color, gray scale or black and white. Under the **View** tab is also where Macros can be viewed. Sorting slides, setting up notes and switching windows can also be accomplished under the **View** tab.

The **Developer** tab (an add-in menu) is for using Macros and Controls. Buttons, check boxes, option buttons and many other controls can be added from the **Developer** tab. The **Developer** tab commands are add-ins that needs to be installed prior to using.

There are special tabs that will only show when using special tools or items such as: Pictures, Shapes, Videos or Text Art. These tabs will show as the last tab in the ribbon and will appear in a different color than the other tabs.

The **Quick Access Toolbar** is located at the top left corner and can be customized to fit your needs. You can add or remove commands from the **Quick Access Toolbar**. You can add to the **Quick Access Toolbar** by going into the **File** tab and *clicking* on **Options** and then **Quick Access Toolbar**. You find the command that you would like to add, highlight it and then push the **Add** button.

Another one of the basics steps that you need to know before we start adding text and pictures is how to add new slides to your presentation. *Click* the **New Slide** button under the **Home** tab. To rearrange the slides, you can *click* on the slide (on the slides directory - on the left side of screen) you want to move and drag up or down. This has not changed since PowerPoint 2003. In PowerPoint 2003, 2007 and 2010 you can *click* on the **View** tab and then *click* on **Slide Sorter**. In **Slide Sorter** you can *click* on the slide you want to move and while holding down the left mouse button *drag* the slide to the location you like. To delete a slide, go to the slide in the slides menu bar on the left side of the screen and *right click* the mouse button. You will see a **Delete Screen Option**.

Now let's get started putting a presentation together. The proper use of PowerPoint to assist you during a presentation can be very powerful in the aid of getting your message across. With the proper amount of text, pictures and objects you can connect with your audience on a higher level, you can articulate your message and you can entertain your audience. Without the aid of PowerPoint it's all up to you. You have to be able to Wow your audience with words and action, something that very few people can do. With too many words, too much animation or not the right color combination you can also lose your audience to confusion or the slide show gets the attention and you take second stage.

In this book I try to give you the tools to do about anything you want to do with PowerPoint, but I also want you to use the tools wisely so you are the presenter and your message is presented in the most dynamic efficient way. When presenting, less is more. The less you have on the slide show the more your audience will pay attention to you. I want you to use PowerPoint to make you look good, and not to make your PowerPoint show dominant the stage.

A good PowerPoint presentation uses the right amount of shapes, pictures, text, and design to emphasize your message. Proper color makes your presentation visually appealing to your audience's eyes. And the proper audio adds excitement to a slide. We can also change color and shape to give the feeling that we want to portray. We add tables, charts, pictures, clip art to give examples to our words. We can add videos to tell stories or have testimonials. And we can add logos, pictures and color to brand our company or ourselves.

I need to warn you about using color. Room lighting and projectors can distort color and make your presentation seem to be black and white. Room lighting can also have an effect on color making some colors blend together that may cause your message to be downplayed. If color is a big part of your message be careful and check over the room and equipment prior to giving your presentation.

In this book you will find that there are many ways to make alterations to the objects in PowerPoint. One of the methods that I do not cover throughout the book is to *right click* on almost any text, table, shape, chart or other object and a short cut tools menu will appear with some of the options to alter the object. If you are having trouble finding the tool in the ribbon, remember to always *right click* the object that you want to alter and see if the tool is in the menu. I also do not cover Macros. I am not a programmer, nor do I ever want to be. Therefore I will not show any VBA script nor talk about programming. I hope this book will be helpful for beginners and pros that want to be more professional in their presentations and for those that want to standout and not give the run-of-the-mill boring PowerPoint presentations that most presenters give.

Throughout the book I have Tips that I hope will either make you more efficient at using PowerPoint or make your presentation unique and stand out. The Tips will be indicated by the icon ☑.

My first tip is to help you get organized and to get started fast.

☑**Tip: Using the Outline tab.**

In normal view use the **Outline** tab on the left side of the screen (instead of the **Slide** view) to type in the titles of new slides. When you hit the **Enter** key a new slide is made. The text you type in the Outline view becomes the title of the new slide. If you use the **Tab** key to indent the title, it becomes a subtitle or a bullet on the slide.

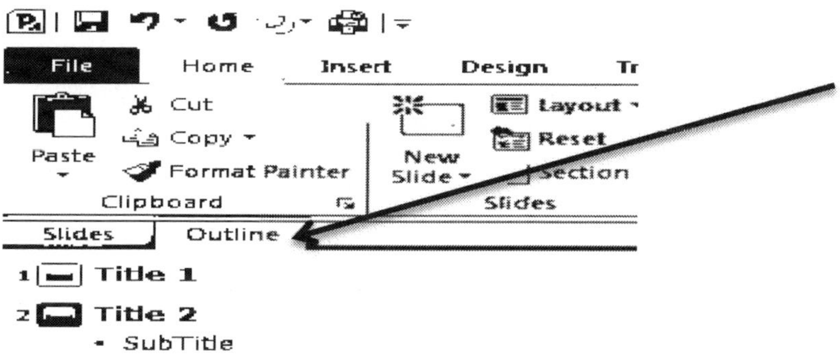

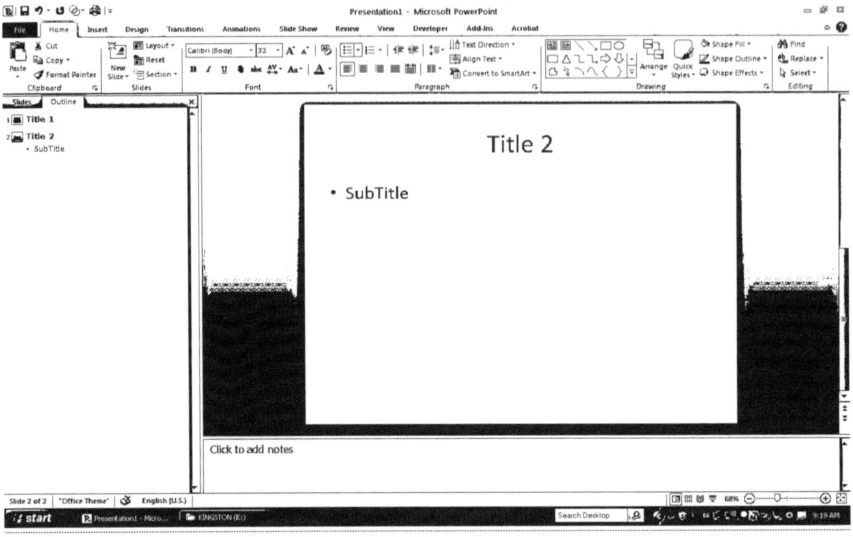

☑Tip: Screen Shortcuts.

There are shortcuts in PowerPoint that help you Zoom-in or Zoom-out on the slide. There are also shortcuts that let you go from one view to another with just a click of the mouse. These are located in the lower right-hand corner of the slide.

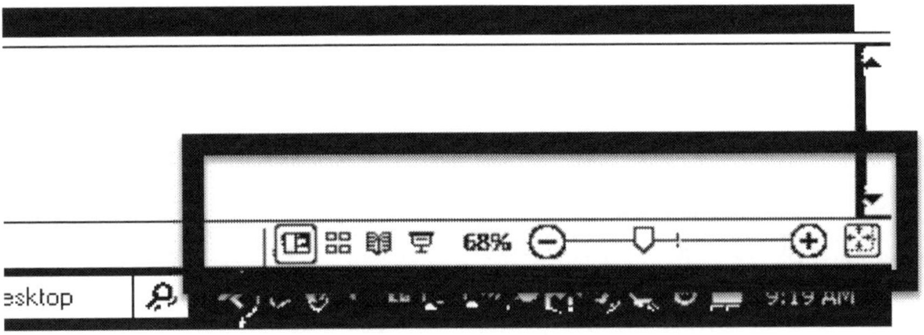

Chapter 2 Add-Ins

Some of the items used in this book are not available from PowerPoint when turned on for the first time. You need to add these additional tools to the ribbon. The menu across the top of the screen is what Microsoft 2010 calls the "Ribbon". Before adding an item to the presentation you first have to add the product to the ribbon. This requires you to install an **Add-In**.

Add-ins can be found under the **File** tab, then **Options**, and then **Add-Ins**. Under the options menu you can also **Customize the Ribbon**, add processes to the **Quick Access Toolbar** and change the **General** options to the ribbon. If you download an add-in or if a co-worker or friend sends you an add-in, you can save it to your computer and then install the add-in by adding it to the available **Add-Ins** list. To install an add-in to the ribbon follow these steps:

1. *Click* the **File** tab.
2. *Click* **Options**.
3. In the **PowerPoint Options** dialog box, *click* **Add-Ins**.
4. In the **Manage** list, (at the bottom of the page) select **Com Add-ins** from the drop down list, and then *click* **Go**. Here you will find add-ins available from other programs that you have installed.
5. Check the box next to the add-in that you want to add.
6. *Click* **OK**.

If you downloaded an **Add-In** or copied one from a friend then follow these steps:

1. *Click* the **File** tab.
2. *Click* **Options**.

3. In the **PowerPoint Options** dialog box, *click* **Add-Ins**.
4. In the **Manage** list, (at the bottom of the page) select **PowerPoint Add-ins** from the drop down list, and then *click* **Go**.
5. In the **Add-Ins** dialog box, *click* **Add New**.
6. In the **Add New PowerPoint Add-In** dialog box, browse for the add-in that you want to add, and then *click* **OK**.
7. A security notice appears. If you are certain that the add-in comes from a trusted source, *click* **Enable Macros**, and then *click* **Close**.

Developer Tab

If you program or use Macros, one of the add-ins that needs to be added to the ribbon is the **Developer** tab. The **Developer** tab is not displayed by default, but you can add it to the ribbon when you want to do or use the following:

1. Write macros.
2. Run macros that you previously recorded.
3. Use XML commands.
4. Use ActiveX controls.
5. Create applications to use with Microsoft Office programs.
6. Use form controls in Microsoft Excel.
7. Work with the **ShapeSheet** in Microsoft Visio.
8. Create new shapes and stencils in Microsoft Visio.

To add the Developer tab to the ribbon follow these steps:

1. *Click* the **File** tab.
2. Under **Help**, *click* **Options**.
3. *Click* **Customize Ribbon**.
4. Under **Customize the Ribbon**, select the **Developer** check box. **Customize the Ribbon** is the right column on the PowerPoint Option dialog window.
5. You may already have the **Developer** selection in the **Main Tabs** group. Then just check the box to add it to the ribbon.
6. You may also need to change the dropdown menu under **Choose commands from:** (the left side column) Change this to **All Commands** to find the **Developer**. Highlight the **Developer** and then under the right column *click* on **New Group**. When a new group appears on the **Main Tabs** list, *click* **Add** to add **Developer** to the new group. *Click* on the new group and then *click* on **Rename** (at the bottom of the page) to rename the group. Then *click* **OK**.

ScreenTips

Microsoft helps you locating the tools you need to use by giving a screen tip when the mouse cursor hovers over a command. There are three levels of help that you can choose from. Follow these steps to select the option that is right for you.

1. *Click* the **File** tab.

2. Under **Help**, *click* **Options**.
3. *Click* **General**.
4. Under **User Interface Options** , in the **ScreenTip style** list, *click* the option that you want:

    - **Show feature descriptions in ScreenTips** This option turns on ScreenTips and Enhanced ScreenTips so that you see more information about a command, including the command name, keyboard shortcuts, art, and links to **Help** articles. This is the default setting.
    - **Don't show feature descriptions in ScreenTips.** This option turns off Enhanced ScreenTips so that you see only the command name and maybe a keyboard shortcut.
    - **Don't show ScreenTips.** This option turns off ScreenTips and Enhanced ScreenTips so that you only see the command name.

Chapter 3 Tables

There are many times when a table will explain your message better than words. PowerPoint lets you custom build a table and alter the table's size, color and overall layout. You can insert tables, draw tables and insert Excel tables.

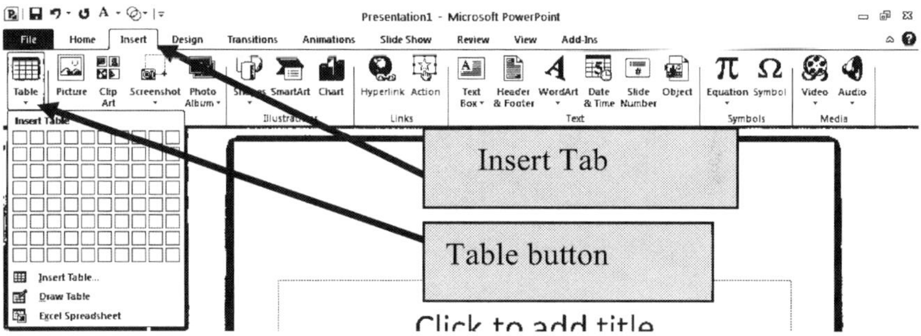

To add tables to the presentation follow these steps:

1. *Click* on the **Insert** tab.
2. *Click* on the **Table** down arrow button. A 10 x 8 diagram shows. This is the number of rows and columns that the table will show. Move your mouse across the diagram to select the number of rows and columns you want. To select the number of rows and columns you want either *click* the lower right box you highlighted or *click* the **Enter** key and the table is inserted on the page.
3. By *right clicking* on the table the number of rows and columns can be changed. Select **Insert** and then select the option you desire.

4. *Click* on a cell in the table that you want to add information and start typing.

When you are working on the table a new ribbon tab appears called **Table Tools**. Under the **Table Tools** tab there are two more tabs **Design** and **Layout**. The **Design** tab is where you can change the look of the table. You can change the table's color, or change individual cell's color. You can also put borders around the cells. You can change the text color here or go to the **Home** tab and change the text color. Under the **Layout** tab you can add rows and columns, split cells, merge cells, change cell size, change the location of the text within the cell, determine the size of the cells and move the table forward or backwards on the page. Under the **Layout** tab are also the tools to align the table. Although the **Group** and **Rotate** tools are dark and seem to be available for tables, they will not work.

Tables inserted this way are not linked to charts. To have tables linked to charts you need to make the chart first and then select the option to show table. This is mostly done in conjunction with Excel.

Moving and Resizing Tables

To move or resize a table, or for that matter any object in PowerPoint (or other Microsoft product) follow these steps:

- To move a table, move the mouse over the table's edge until the mouse pointer has a four arrow cross hair appear. Then *click and drag* to the location you desire.

- To resize the table, move the mouse over the table's edge (or at the corner of the table), until the mouse pointer has a double arrow line. Then *click and drag* to the size you desire.

- Hold down the Ctrl key to keep the center point of the table in the same location. When holding down the Ctrl key while moving an edge, the opposite side of the table will also move outward or inward, depending on if you are enlarging or shrinking the table.

Make sure that the table is selected or you will not see the more or resize arrows. If more than one table or object is selected all the objects will move of be resized.

Change Row or Column Size

To change a row or column's width or height, move the mouse cursor over the border between the two columns or rows that you want to change. Two parallel lines with arrows appear, *click* on the line (border) and *drag* the line to the size that you want. If you want to change all the cell's height or width then follow these steps:

1. *Click* on the *table.*
2. *Click* on the **Table Tools – Layout** tab.
3. Under the **Table Size** group, change the **Height** or **Width** number in the text box.

If you want to keep the same aspect ratio while you change the cell or table size, check the box next to **Lock Aspect Ratio**, which is located under the **Table Tools Layout** tab, in the **Table Size** group.

Insert Rows & Columns

Once you have inserted a table to the page you can alter the table by adding rows or columns.

1. *Click* on the table that you want to add a row or column.

2. *Click* on a cell that you want to add a row or column next to.
3. *Click* on **Table Tools – Layout**.
4. Then select one of the following in the **Rows & Columns** group.

   A. **Insert Above**. This will insert a row above the selected cell. The new row will be the same size and color as the selected cell's row.

   B. **Insert Below**. This will insert a row below the selected cell. The new row will be the same size and color as the selected cell's row.

   C. **Insert Left**. This will insert a row to the left of the selected cell. The new row will be the same size and color as the selected cell's row.

   D. **Insert Right**. This will insert a row to the right of the selected cell. The new row will be the same size and color as the selected cell's row.

Note that there will only be one header row, and the color for a header row is mostly a lighter or darker color than the other rows in the table. Also color will vary depending on the table style that has been chosen.

Deleting Rows & Columns

If you find that you have too many rows or columns it is easy to remove them from the table.

1. *Click* on a cell of the table that is either in the row or the column that you would like to delete.

2. *Click* on **Table Tools – Layout** tab.
3. Under the **Rows & Columns** group, *click* on **Delete**.
4. *Click* on one of the following:

   A. **Delete Columns**. This will delete the column that contained the cell you selected in step 2.
   B. **Delete Rows**. This will delete the row that contained the cell you selected in step 2.
   C. **Delete Table**. This deletes the complete table.

Change Colors in Tables

To change the color of the complete table *click* on the **Table Tools –Design** tab. Under the **Table Styles** group there are many theme colors to choose from. By *clicking* on the **More** arrow, a wide selection of colored table themes are available. *Click* on the color layout that you would like and the table on the slide changes.

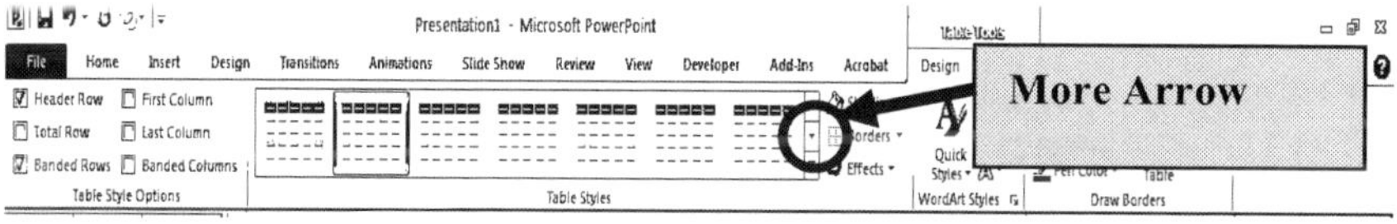

To change the color of one or more cells,

1. Either *click* in the single cell or select several cells by *clicking* in the upper left cell where you want the color change to begin and *drag* the mouse to the lower right cell where you want the color change to end.
2. *Click* the **Table Tools – Design** tab.

3. *Click* **Shading** in the **Table Style** group.
4. A **Theme Colors** dialog box opens. *Click* the color that you would like to have.
5. If you do not see the color you want, select **More Fill Colors.**
6. A Color dialog window opens. You can select a different color under the **Standard** tab or you can adjust the color under the **Custom** tab.

You can also change the **Texture** or the **Gradient** of the color under **Shading**.

If you want to insert a picture in a cell, you can do that under the Shading command also.

1. *Click* on the table
2. *Click* on the cell that you would like to insert the picture.
3. *Click* on **Table Tools – Design** tab.
4. *Click* on **Shading** under the **Table Styles** group.
5. Go down the list and *click* on **Picture**.
6. The **Insert Picture** dialog window will open. Find the picture that you want to insert. *Click* on the picture.
7. *Click* **Insert**.
8. The picture is now in the cell of the table.

To add a texture or a gradient color, do the following:

1. *Click* on the table
2. *Click* on the cell that you would like to insert the texture or the gradient color.

3. *Click* on **Table Tools – Design** tab.
4. *Click* on **Shading** under the **Table Styles** group.
5. Go down the list and *click* on either **Texture** or **Gradient**.
6. If you *clicked* **Texture,** a texture sample window opens. You can select one of the textures in the sample list or you can *click* **More Textures** at the bottom of the window.
7. If you *clicked* on **More Textures** the **Format Shape** dialog window opens. Here you can make detail changes to the cell.
8. If you *clicked* **Gradient,** a gradient dialog window opens the shows different shades of gradients. You can choose one of the samples or you can go to the bottom of the dialog window and *click* on **More Gradients.**
9. If you *clicked* on **More Gradients**, the **Format Shape** dialog window opens. Here you can make detail changes to the cell.

If you add a texture, gradient or picture and then change the **Table Style** in the **Table Tools – Design** tab, the texture, gradient or picture will be replaced with the color of the **Table Styles** example color.

You can also change the color of the Header Row, Total Row, Banded Rows, First Column, Last Column and Banded Column with just a *click* of the mouse.

1. *Click* on the table.
2. *Click* on **Table Tools – Design**.

3. Under the **Table Style Options** group check the boxes of the row or column that you would like to change the color.
    a. As you change the theme color in the **Table Style** group the example in the **Table Style Options** color will match to show the changes.

Table Effects

You can add bevels, shadows or reflections to cells of a table also.

1. *Click* on the cell that you want to add the effect to or if you want to add the effect to the complete table, make sure that the table is selected and not a single cell.
2. *Click* on **Table Tools –Design** tab.
3. *Click* on **Effects** in the **Table Styles** group.
4. *Click* on either: **Cell Bevel, Shadow** or **Reflection**. A dialog window opens with a variety of bevels, shadows or reflections.
5. *Click* on the style of bevel, shadow or reflection that you would like.
6. Note that shadow or reflection may not show for individual cells.

Splitting a Cell

If you would like to split a cell into two or more cells:

1. Select the table.
2. *Click* **Table Tools – Design** tab.
3. *Click* **Draw Table** tab under the **Draw Borders** group. Once you *click* on the **Draw Table** tab the mouse cursor turns to a pin.
4. Go to the cell that you would like to split. *Click* on the left border of the cell that you want to split, and then *drag* to the right border. You can also *click and drag* the pen from top to bottom to split the cell vertically.
5. The cell then splits into two cells.

If you would like to draw a diagonal line across the cell use the same process except *click* in a corner of the cell and *drag* to the opposite corner. This does not slit the cells, but it will draw a line across the cell. To change the pen back to an arrow; either *click* outside the table or push the **A** key.

You can change the color of the line by picking a color under the **Pen Color** tab, which is also located in the **Draw Border** group under the **Table Tools – Design** tab.

You can also split cells by using the layout tab.

1. Select the table.
2. *Click* on **Table Tools – Layout** tab.
3. *Click* on a cell or a combination of cells.
4. Under the **Merge** group, *click* on split cell.

5. A **Split Cells** dialog window opens. Select the Number of Columns and the Number of Rows that you would like to have after the split.
6. *Click* **OK**.

Merge Cells

If you need to merge two or more cells, this can be done with the eraser.

1. *Click* on **Table Tools – Design** tab.
2. *Click* on **Eraser** in the **Draw Borders** group. A small eraser will replace the mouse arrow.
3. Move the eraser to the border that is between the cells you want to join. *Click* on the line (border).
4. The line will disappear.

If the table is small you may have a hard time selecting the border that you want to erase. You can enlarge the table to select the border easier, and then resize the table once the border is erased, or you can use the Zoom In and Zoom Out slider bar located in the lower right hand corner of the slide. *Click* outside the table or push the **A** key to change the eraser back to an arrow.

You can also merge cells under the layout tab.

1. Select the table.
2. *Click* on **Table Tools – Layout** tab.
3. *Click* on the first cell and *drag* your mouse to the other cells that you would like to merge. All the cells should be highlighted.
4. *Click* on **Merge Cells** under the **Merge** group.

5. The cells merge.

Changing Border Colors

If you would like to put a colored border around a cell in a table or put different colors for each border follow these steps.

1. *Click* on the Table that you want to alter.
2. *Click* **Table Tools – Design**.
3. Under the **Draw Borders** group, *click* the **Pen Color**. A **Theme Color** dialog menu appears.
4. *Click* the color that you would like the border to be. The mouse cursor turns to a pen.
5. Move the cursor (pen) over the border that you want to change, and *click* on the border. The border changes color.
6. If you have used the Bevel option on the cells the border color may not be apparent.

By changing the line options above the **Pen Color** in the **Draw Borders** group, you can change the thickness and style of the border.

1. *Click* on the table.
2. *Click* on **Table Tools – Design**.
3. *Click* on the drop down arrow above the **Pen Color** option. This is the **Pen Weight** box.
4. *Click* on the thickness you desire.
5. The mouse cursor will change to a pen. Move the mouse to the border that you would like to change the thickness, and *click* the border.

6. If you would like to have a dotted line for a border instead of a solid line, *click* on the first drop down list box in the **Draw Borders** group, this is the **Pen Style** box. A drop down list of different dotted line options appears.
7. *Click* on the line option that you would like.
8. The mouse arrow cursor changes to a pen. Move the pen over the border you would like to change and *click*.

To change the pen back to an arrow; either *click* outside the table or push the **A** key.

Chapter 4 Pictures

Instead of using text to get your message across, try using pictures. Some of the most effective presenters use pictures instead of words. It is considered taboo to use PowerPoint slides as notes or to read the PowerPoint slides. Therefore using pictures is a good idea.

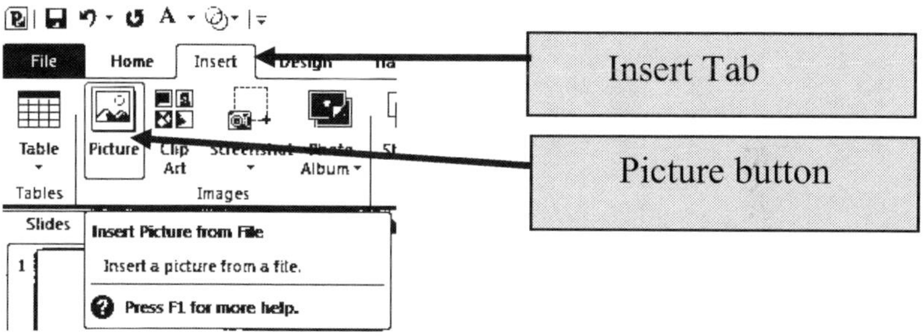

To add a pictures to the presentation follow these steps:

1. *Click* on **Insert** tab.
2. *Click* on **Picture**, an **Insert Picture** dialog window will appear. Mostly this will be the pictures' that you have added to the **My Pictures** file. You can select any file that has pictures in them, and then select the picture you would like to add.
3. *Click* **Insert** at the bottom of the window.
4. The picture is now on the presentation page.

Moving and Changing the Size of Pictures

- To move a picture, move the mouse over the table's edge until the mouse pointer has a four arrow cross hair appear. Then *click and drag* to the location you desire.

- To resize the picture, move the mouse over the table's edge (or at the corner of the table), until the mouse pointer has a double arrow line. Then *click and drag* to the size you desire.
    - Hold down the Ctrl key to keep the center point of the picture in the same location. When holding down the Ctrl key while moving an edge, the opposite side of the table will also move outward or inward, depending on if you are enlarging or shrinking the table.

Change the Picture's Shape

PowerPoint lets you change the shape of a picture. This can add character to your presentation. If you want to change the shape of a picture follow these steps:

1. *Click* the picture. A new special menu bar called **Picture Tools**, show up at the top of the page.
2. *Click* the **Picture Tools - Format** tab.
3. *Click* on **Crop** dropdown arrow. A drop down menu will appear.
4. *Click* on **Crop to Shape**.
5. *Click* on the shape that you want and the pictures outline will be redesigned to the shape.

Inserting a Picture in WordArt

Adding pictures to text is a very artistic way to get a message across with both words and pictures. To insert pictures inside the text you can use WordArt or just text. To use WordArt follow these steps:

1. *Click* **Insert**
2. *Click* **WordArt**. Consider one of the following:
    a. If you want the text to have a border, select a WordArt that only shows an outline of the letter. The color of the outline will show around the picture, therefore coordinating the outline color and the picture is important.
    b. If you don't want the text to have a border, select a WordArt that is solid. Generally the color of WordArt you select should not matter.
3. Select the **WordArt** you like.
4. Type your text.
5. Size the WordArt to the desired size. Make the WordArt big enough that the picture will show in the text. Make sure that the text is highlighted before going on to the next step.
6. To resize **WordArt** do the following:
7. Highlight the text.
8. *Click* on **Home**
9. Under the **Font** group, either continue to *click* on the large **A** or the small **A** to enlarge or shrink. You

can also *click* on the **Font Size** drop down box, and either enter a fonts size or select a fonts size from the drop down list. Once again make sure that the text is highlighted.

10. *Click* on **Drawing Tools – Format**.
11. In the **WordArt Styles** group *click* on **Text Fill**. A **Theme Colors** dialog window opens.
12. *Click* on **Picture**. An **Insert Picture** dialog window opens.
13. Look through your files to find the right picture.
14. *Click* on the picture of your choice.
15. *Click* **Insert**. The picture now is in the text.

If you want to insert a picture in text, the text has to be big enough to allow a picture to be shown in the text. Follow these steps for inserting a picture in the text:

1. Make sure the text is big and bold.
2. *Click* on **Drawing Tools – Format**.
3. Under the **WorkArt Styles** group, *click* on the drop down arrow next to the **Text Fill** box.
4. Select **Picture**. The **Insert Picture** dialog window opens
5. Look through your files to find the right picture.
6. *Click* on the picture of your choice.
7. *Click* **Insert**. The picture now is in the text.

Group or Ungroup Pictures

You can group shapes, pictures, or other objects. Grouping lets you rotate, flip, move, or resize all shapes or objects at the same time as though they were a single item. You can also change the attributes of all of the items in a group at one time, by adding a picture effect or color for example. You can select an item within a group and apply an attribute without ungrouping the shapes, or you can create groups within groups to help you build complex drawings.
To group pictures, shapes or objects together follow these steps:

1. *Click* on a picture or shape.
2. *Control (Ctrl) Click* the second picture or shape. *Control (Ctrl) Click* any other item that you would like to add to the group.
3. Under the **Picture Tools - Format** tab (this may also be a **Drawing Tools – Format** tab), *click* the **Group** dropdown menu.
4. *Click* **Group**

Now you can make your changes. Move, change color or add effects. If the picture has been changed to a shape using the crop tool you may not be able to group it with other pictures.

If you do not see the **Picture Tools** or **Format** tabs, make sure that you selected a shape or other object. You might have to *double-click* the object to open the **Format** tab. After you group pictures or other objects, you can continue to select any single picture or object within the group. Select the group, and then *click* the individual picture or object that you want to select.

You can also ungroup a group of shapes at any time and then regroup them later.

Ungroup Pictures

To ungroup a group of shapes, pictures, or other objects (for example, if you want to move a group but leave one shape behind or make extensive changes to one shape without changing the other shapes), do the following:

1. Select the group that you want to ungroup.
2. *Click* on **Picture Tools - Format** tab, in the Arrange group.
3. *Click* on **Group** dropdown arrow.
4. *Click* **Ungroup**.

If you do not see the **Drawing Tools**, **Picture Tools**, or **Format** tabs, make sure that you selected a group of shapes, pictures, or other objects. You might have to *double-click* the object to open the **Format** tab.

Regroup pictures

To regroup items that were previously grouped and then ungrouped, do the following:

1. Select anyone of the pictures or objects that was previously in a group.
2. Select **Picture Tools - Format** tab.
3. In the **Arrange** group, *click* **Group**.
4. *Click* **Regroup**.

If you do not see the **Picture Tools** or **Format** tabs, make sure that you selected a picture or other object. You might have to *double-click* the object to open the **Format** tab.

The Group button is not available

The **Group** button may not be available if the shape, picture or object has been inserted into a placeholder or you are trying to group a placeholder, as placeholders cannot be grouped with other shapes, pictures, objects.

You might have to move the shape, picture, or object to another location on your slide outside of the placeholder or remove the placeholder from the objects that you want to use the group function.

The **Group** button may also not be available if the picture has been altered using the **Crop – Crop to Shape** tool.

Stacked Objects

When objects on a slide are stacked on top of each other, it can be difficult to select individual objects. For example, you might want to select one object to apply a custom effect, but it is buried under other items. Use the **Selection and Visibility** task pane to select that object. To open the **Selection and Visibility** pane follow these steps:

1. *Click* the **Home** tab.
2. In the **Editing** group, *click* **Select**. The **Editing** group is mostly located to the far right of the ribbon.
3. *Click* **Selection Pane**. The **Selection and Visibility** pane opens.
4. *Click* on the item you would like to select. The item is highlighted on the presentation page.

After you have selected the object, you can apply PowerPoint commands and features to that object as usual. If the **Selection and Visibility** pane is large enough there will be boxes with eye icons in them to the right of the list of shapes. By *clicking* on the eye icon you can hide or unhide the shape or object on the slide. If the eye icons are not visible, move the mouse over the edge between the slide and the **Selection and Visibility** pane.

When the mouse cursor changes to a double arrow line, *click and drag* the edge to the left. This should expose the eye icons.

Moving Forward or Backwards

If you want to move the picture forward (above the other objects) do the following:

In the **Selection and Visibility** pane that was opened in the previous section, select the picture that you would like to move forward or send backwards. Then do one of the following:

- At the bottom of the **Selection and Visibility** pane, *click* on the up or down arrows to move the picture forward or backwards.
- *Click* on **Picture Tools – Format**. Under the Arrange group *click* on the **Bring Forward** button or the **Send Backward** button.

Pictures as Watermarks

PowerPoint does a terrible job making a picture a watermark that lies on the top of the slide. A PNG file format picture seems to work better than a JPEG file format picture. I like using shapes or text for watermarking a presentation, instead of pictures.

For a PNG format picture do the following:

1. To make a PNG picture a watermark *Click* the slide that you want to add a watermark to.
2. *Click* on **Picture Tools – Format**.
3. *Click* on **Corrections** dropdown arrow. A **Brightness and Contrast** example box shows up.

4. At the bottom of the box *click* on **Picture Corrections Options.**
5. *Click* the **Glow and Soft Edges** tab.
6. Under the **Soft Edges** section *click* on the dropdown arrow next to **Presets.**
7. Set the soft edges to **25 Points**. Or the level that you desire. This setting will vary from picture to picture.
8. *Click* **Close.**
9. Under the **Picture Tools – Format** tab, in the **Arrange** group, select **Bring Forward** to bring the new watermarked picture to the top level.

For a JPEG format picture do the following:

1. To make a JPEG picture a watermark, c*lick* the slide that you want to add a watermark to.
2. *Click* on **Picture Tools – Format**.
3. *Click* on **Corrections** dropdown arrow. A **Brightness and Contrast** example box shows up.
4. At the bottom of the box *click* on **Picture Corrections Options.**
5. *Click* the **Picture Correction** tab.
6. Move the **Brightness** slider over to the right to make the picture fade to the degree that you would like.
7. *Click* **Close.**
8. Make sure that the picture is still selected.
9. Under the **Picture Tools – Format** tab, in the **Arrange** group, do one of the following:

- If the picture is on top of other objects, select **Bring Forward** to move the new watermarked picture to the top level.
- If the picture is on the background, with no other objects that would cover the watermark, select **Send Backward** to move the new watermarked picture to the bottom level.

The JPEG format is not transparent and makes a terrible watermark.

Putting watermarks on every slide

To add a watermark to all of the slides in a blank presentation, on the **View** tab, in the **Master Views** group, *click* **Slide Master**.

If your completed presentation contains one or more master slide, you might not want to apply the watermarked picture to the master slides and risk unwanted changes to your presentation. The safe alternative is to add the background to one slide at a time. Also, using a picture as a watermark in PowerPoint is not a good choice for watermarking a presentation.

1. On the **Insert** tab, in the **Images** group, do one of the following:
    a. To use a picture as a watermark, *click* **Picture**, locate the picture that you want, and then *click* **Insert**.
    b. To use clip art as a watermark, *click* **Clip Art.** In the **Clip Art** task pane, in the **Search for** box, either type a word or phrase that describes the clip that you want, or type all

or part of the file name of the clip, and then *click* **Go**.

2. To adjust the size of the picture or clip art, *right-click* the picture or clip art on the slide, and then *click* **Size and Position** on the shortcut menu.
3. In the **Size** pane, under **Scale**, increase or decrease the settings in the **Height** and **Width** boxes.
4. To maintain proportional height and width of the picture or clip art when scaling, select the **Lock Aspect Ratio** check box.
5. To move the picture or clip art on the slide, *click* the **Position** tab, and then enter the settings for the positions that you want in the **Horizontal** and **Vertical** boxes.
6. To recolor the picture, *click* **Picture Color** tab, and then under **Recolor**, *click* the color fade that you want.
7. If you want to change the brightness and contrast, *click* **Picture Correction**, and then under **Brightness and Contrast**, move the slider bar to the brightness percentage that you want.
8. When you finish editing and positioning the watermark and are satisfied with its appearance, *click* **Close**.
9. To send the watermark to the back of the slide, under **Picture Tools - Format** tab, in the **Arrange** group, *click* the arrow next to **Send Backward**, and then *click* **Send to Back**.

Changing Color of a Picture

In PowerPoint you can alter the picture by changing the color or adding effects to the picture.

1. *Click* on the picture.
2. *Click* on **Picture Tools – Format** tab.
3. Under the **Adjust** group, *click* **Color**. A **Color Saturation** dialog window opens.
4. You can make changes to:
   a. **Color Saturation**. The saturation is scaled from 0% to 400%
   b. **Color Tone.** This is given in Temperature xxxxx K.
   c. **Recolor**. Changes color tent of the picture.
   d. **More Variation.** This opens a Theme Color dialog window.
   e. **Set Transparent Color**. This lets you select one color on the picture and makes it transparent. Only one color can be transparent on a picture.
   f. **Picture Color Options**. This opens a Format Picture dialog window, with detailed options to change the picture.

☑**Tip: Getting the color just right**

When you need to get the color as close as possible, you may need to use a third party software to find the RGB color numbers. The RGB numbers range from 0 to 255 for each color (Red, Green and Blue). You can find third party software online for free or at a low cost. Most use a dropper or magnifying class icon to find the RGB numbers, that you click on and then move your mouse over the color that you are trying to find the RGB for and the RBG numbers are calculated for you. Just copy these RGB numbers into the **More Fill Colors** dialog box, under the **Custom** tab. I use a free third party color finder called Color Cop (http://www.colorcop.net). The owner of the site asks for a donation. I have found this software is easy to use and pretty accurate. You do have to remember that the color of your slides will change from screen to screen and change even more when using projectors.

Sharpen, Soften, or Change Brightness and Contrast.

You can make pictures sharper or softer by using the **Corrections** tools. Under the **Corrections** tool is also the option to brighten pictures.

1. *Click* on the picture.
2. *Click* on **Picture Tools – Format** tab.
3. Under the **Adjust** group, *click* **Corrections**.
4. The **Sharpen and Soften** dialog window opens.

   Here you can make changes to the pictures contrast by adjusting the tone of the picture.

The **Artistic Effects** tab can add further effects to the picture. Under the **Artistic Effects** are options for Pencil Grayscale, Line Drawing, Blur, Paint Strokes, Chalk Sketch, Light Screen, Watercolor Sponge, Film Grain, Glass and many more.

Picture Borders

PowerPoint let you frame pictures and then change the color of the frame.

1. *Click* on the picture.
2. *Click* on the **Picture Tools – Format** tab.
3. Under the **Picture Styles** group, *click* the **More** drop down arrow in the lower right corner of the picture style examples.

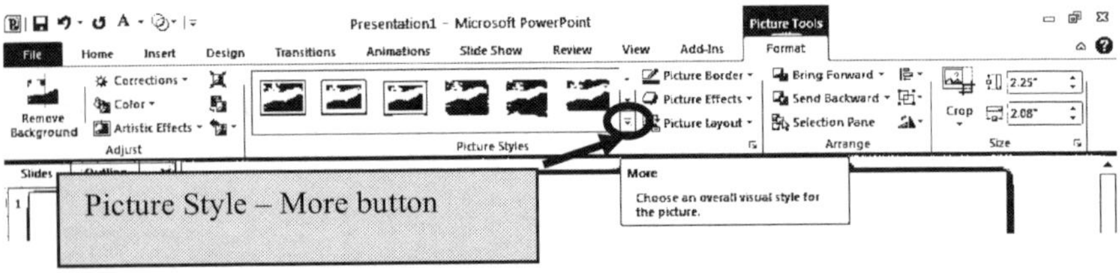

4. Select the picture – frame style that you want. Notice that there are options that let you select picture effects such as bevel, rotate, round curved corners, tilt and more. There are examples with white borders or black borders.

To change the <u>Color of the border</u>, do the following:

1. *Click* on the picture.
2. *Click* on the **Picture Tools – Format** tab.
3. Under the **Picture Styles** group, *click* on **Picture Borders.**
4. A **Theme Colors** dialog window opens. Select the color you want.

To change the <u>Thickness of the border,</u> do the following:

1. *Click* on the picture.
2. *Click* on the **Picture Tools – Format** tab.
3. Under the **Picture Styles** group, *click* on **Picture Borders.**

4. *Click* on **Weight**. Select the weight of the border you like.

Aligning Pictures

Many times it is hard to get pictures, shapes or text boxes to line up in a straight row or column. PowerPoint makes it easy to align objects.

1. *Click* on the first object; weather a picture, shape, text box or chart.
2. Use either the *Shift – Click* method or the *Ctrl – Click* method to select all the objects that you want to align.
3. *Click* on the **Drawing Tools – Format** tab.
4. Under the **Arrange** group, *click* on **Align**.
5. The **Align** list appears, select the alignment that you would like.

Animating Pictures

There may be very few times that you need or want to animate a picture. During an introduction of a video or when you want to have a photo album type of slide show might be examples of when you would like to animate pictures. Animating pictures is simple and somewhat limited compare to charts and SmartArt.

A word on animations: With all animation caution should be taken. Too much animation can make the audience watching the animation and not paying attention to you. I have seen where wild fast moving animations have made the audience dizzy and therefore not enjoy the presentation. So use animations wisely.

1. *Click* on the picture.
2. *Click* the **Animations** tab.
3. In the **Animation** group select the animation you would like.
4. For additional animation effects *click* the drop down arrow on the right side of the animation example. Animations are broken into groups of entrances, emphasis, exits and motion paths. Note that entrance animations are noted in green, emphasis animations are noted in yellow and exit animations are noted in red.
5. *Click* the animation you would like. If the picture is visible, once the mouse is hovering over the animation the picture will play the animation, showing the animation of the picture.
6. *Click* on the animation of your choice. The picture now has a number next to it in the upper left corner. This number is the animation sequence number for the page.

Set the animation effect options

To set the animation effect options, do the following:

1. Select the animated picture that you want to modify.
2. *Click* the **Animations** tab, in the **Animations** group.
3. *Click* the **Effect Options** button that is to the right of the animation examples.

4. A drop down list appears that give you option for the particular animation you have chosen. For example if you had a Wipe animation the **Effect Options** might give you the option to wipe from the bottom, wipe from the left, wipe from the right or wipe from the top.

Another way to change the effects of an animated picture is to open the **Animation Pane**. To change the effects in the **Animation Pane** do the following:

1. *Click* on the animated picture.
2. *Click* on the **Animations** tab.
3. *Click* **Animation Pane** under the **Advanced Animation** group.

In the **Animation Pane** list, *click* the drop down arrow to the right of the animation that you want to modify.

1. Select **Effect Options**.
2. In the dialog box, on the **Effect** tab, in the **Settings** group, *click* the **Direction** box.
3. Select the effect option you would like.

Animation Painter

One of the new features in Microsoft PowerPoint 2010 is the Animation Painter. Using the Animation Painter, you can easily and quickly copy an animation or several animations from one object to another.

To copy animations from one object to another, do the following:

1. Select the object (picture, shape or text) with the animations that you want to copy.

2. On the **Animations** tab, in the **Advanced Animation** group, *click* **Animation Painter**.
3. *Click* the chart that you want to copy the animations onto.
4. The animation is now copied to the new object.

Remove an Animation

If you no longer want a picture to be animated follow these steps:

1. *Click* on the picture with the animation that you want to remove.
2. On the **Animations** tab, in the **Animation** group *click* **None**. If you don't see **None**, *click* the drop down arrow on the right side of the animation example for more options. **None** is mostly the top option.

Timing or Effect Options for Pictures

You can customize the timing of animation effects in Microsoft PowerPoint 2010, including the timing and order with which they start, and whether they repeat.

To set the start time for an animation effect, follow these steps:

1. *Click* on the picture that you want to set the timing.
2. On the **Animations** tab, in the **Timing** group, do one of the following:

3. To start the animation effect when you *click* the slide, select **Start:** On Click
4. To start the animation effect at the same time as the previous effect in the list (that is, one click executes multiple animation effects), select **Start:** With Previous
5. To start the animation effect immediately after the previous effect in the list finishes playing (that is, you do not have to click again to make the next animation effect start), select **Start:** After Previous

Changing the Duration or Delaying the start of an Animation Effect

1. *Click* on the picture that contains the animation effect for which you want to set a delay or other timing option.
2. On the **Animations** tab, in the **Timing** group, do one or more of the following:
   a. To specify the length of an animation effect, enter a number in the **Duration** box.
   b. To create a delay between the end of one animation effect and the start of a new animation effect, enter a number in the **Delay** box.

Repeat or rewind an animation effect

You can make an animation repeat a number of times (2, 3, 4, 5, or 10 times), **Until Next Click**, or **until end of slide**. To make an animation effect or sequence of effects repeat or return to its original position, follow these steps:

1. *Click* on the picture that you want the animation to repeat.
2. On the **Animations** tab, in the **Animation** group, *click* on the arrow in the lower right-hand corner of the Animation group box. This is called **Show Additional Effect Options** launcher.
3. A new window appears, *click* the **Timing** tab, and then do one or more of the following:
   a. To select a repeat option *click* on the **Repeat** drop down arrow, and select an option in the **Repeat** list.
   b. To automatically return an animation effect to its original look and location after it plays, select the **Rewind when done playing** check box.

Changing the Order of Animations

Animated objects on a slide display a number indicating the order in which the object's animation plays. When there are two or more animation effects, you can change the order in which each plays by doing one of the following:

- On the slide, *click* an animation that you want to move up or down in the sequence, and then *click* on the **Animations** tab, in the **Timing** group, under **Reorder Animation**, *click* **Move Earlier** or **Move Later**.

- On the **Animations** tab, in the **Advanced Animation** group, *click* **Animation Pane**. You can change the order by *dragging* objects up or down in the list, or *click* on the item you want to move and then use the **Re-Order** arrows at the bottom of the **Animation Pane**. You can also *click* an object in the **Animation Pane** and then in the **Timing** group, under **Reorder Animation**, *click* **Move Earlier** or **Move Later**.

Trigger an Animation Effect

With triggers, you can make an animation effect occur during a slide show when you *click* an object on the slide or when you play a specific part of a video.

Set a trigger on click

1. Select the picture or object that has the animation that you want to trigger.
2. On the **Animations** tab, in the **Advanced Animation** group, *click* **Trigger**.
3. *Click* **On Click of**, and select the object that you want to trigger the animation.

Disable animations from playing in Slide Show

1. *Click* on the **Slide Show** tab.
2. Under the **Set Up** group, *click* **Set Up Slide Show**.

3 In the **Set Up Show** dialog box, under **Show options**, select the **Show without animation** check box.

4 *Click* **OK**.

☑ Tip: Making a Silhouette from a picture

Silhouettes are very popular and can be used to doll-up your presentation. First find a picture of a person. Or take a picture of yourself (don't care how you look, we will never know that the silhouette is you).

1. First insert the picture into the slide. (See the instructions at the beginning of the Pictures chapter).
2. With the picture selected, you first need to remove background.
3. Under **Picture Tools – Format**, *click* on **Remove Background.** If the picture is a PNG file, the background may already be removed.
4. Use the **Mark Areas to Keep** and **Mark Areas to Remove** to remove the background and unwanted items.
5. Now you should have a picture of a person without any cluster. Make sure the picture is selected.
6. *Click* on **Corrections** under the **Picture Tools – Format** tab in the **Adjust** group.
7. Go down to the bottom of the list and *click* on **Picture Corrections Options**.

8. In the **Picture Corrections** tab, under the **Brightness and Contrast** section, move the **Brightness** slider bar all the way to the left.
9. *Click* **Close**. The picture is now a silhouette.
10. *Right click* on the picture and *click* on **Save as Picture**. Name the picture and now you have a silhouette picture.

☑Tip: Silhouette picture as a bullet

One of the neat things to use this new silhouette picture for is, bullets in text boxes.

1. Select a bullet text box.
2. Under the **Home** tab, in the **Paragraph** group, *click* on the drop down arrow next to the **Bullets** icon.
3. Select **Bullets and Numbering** at the bottom of the dialog box.
4. When the **Bullets and Numbering** dialog window opens, select **Pictures**.
5. Find the silhouette picture you just made and *click* **OK**. Now the boring bullet has changed to a dynamic silhouette.
6. The boring bullets have changed to a modern highly desired silhouette.

Chapter 5 Clip Art

There are animated clip art available on PowerPoint, you can also get animated clip art from the Internet, or make them yourself with third party software. If you downloaded a clip art or made the clip art yourself it may not be in the PowerPoint clip art file and therefore not show up when you *click* **Insert-Clip Art**. In this case you have to insert the animated clips art by using the **Insert – Picture** tab instead of the **Insert – Clip Art** tab (both under the Images group).

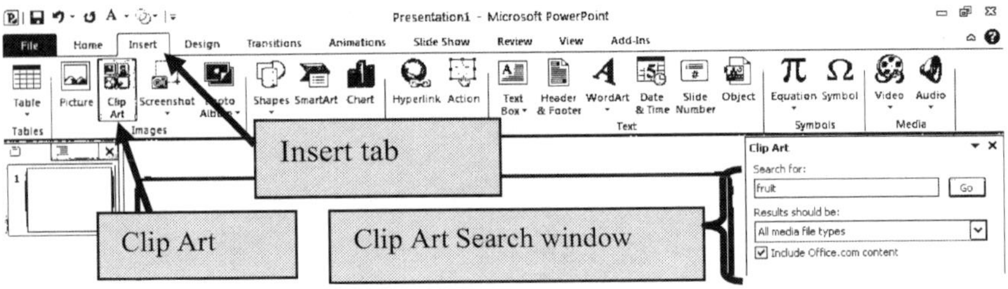

To insert clip art follow these steps:

1. *Click* on **Insert**.
2. *Click* on **Clip Art**. The **Clip Art** search window opens.
3. In the **Search For** text box, type a description of the clip art you are looking for. For example: Men. Examples of clip art that include men are displayed.
4. Either *double-click* on the clip are or *click* on the drop down arrow on the right side of the clip art and *click* on **Insert**.

Types of Clip Art

Clip art comes in different file formats, such as WMF, JPG, PNG, or GIF. To determine what type of file the clip art is, move your mouse over the clip art in the clip art search pane. Or *click* on the drop down arrow on the right side of the clip art (in the **Clip Art** search pane). Then *click* on **Preview Properties**. The Type is shown in the **Preview Properties** dialog window. There are different things that you can do with the different file formats.

WMF Images

With a WMF image you can ungroup parts of the clip art, but first you must convert it to a Microsoft Office drawing object. When you select the clip art go to the **Group** button in the **Picture Tools – Format** tab, in the **Arrange** group. *Click* on the drop down arrow next to **Group** and *click* on **Ungroup**. A Microsoft PowerPoint dialog window will open asking you if you would like to change the clip art to a Microsoft Office drawing object. *Click* **Yes** and now the clip art is broken up into sections. To see all the separated sections, you need to **Ungroup** the clip art again. Now the clip art has white circles and squares all over the clip art. Each section can be cut, copied, deleted, moved, resized, rotated or changed to a different color. If you have **Ungrouped** the clip art, there may be too many white circles and squared to know where to begin. Click off the picture, and then click on specific parts of the picture. Or *click and drag* to select groups of the picture. **Group** the clip art back together so the picture can be moved and sized as a whole.

JPG Image

A JPG clip art is similar to a picture. It cannot be ungrouped, but it can be rotated, sized, cropped and altered using the **Corrections**, **Color** and **Artistic Effects** tools. Mostly a JPG image has a background. The background can be removed per the instructions in the picture chapter.

PNG Image
A PNG clip art is similar to a picture. It cannot be ungrouped, but it can be rotated, sized, cropped and altered using the **Corrections**, **Color** and **Artistic Effects** tools. Many PNG images do not have backgrounds and can easily be altered to a silhouette.

GIF Image
GIF images are mostly animated files. Some section of the image moves in some sort of fashion. Gif images cannot be broken into sections like WMF image can. Also when you enlarge a GIF image they can get distorted because they are pixelate - bitmap pictures not vector pictures. GIF animation only takes place in the Slide Show view not in the Normal view.

Some WMG, JPG and PNG images can be enlarged without distorting. Mostly it depends if the image is a Bitmap or a Vector format. Some common bitmap formats are BMP, GIF, JPEG, JPG, and PNG. Some common vector formats are AI, CDR, CMX, CGM, DXF and WMF. Vector format files can be enlarged without distortion.
If you use an animated clip art character you may have to animate the animated clip art to have the clip art move over the page. For example you would like to have an animated clip art cartoon character walk across the screen. The animated clip art may appear to be walking but is not moving. You have to add the motion by adding a Motion Path animation, and then character appears to be walking across the screen.
To animate the clip art across the screen follow these steps.

1. *Click* on the animated clip art.
2. *Click* on **Animations**.
3. *Click* on the **More** drop down arrow in the lower right corner of the animation examples, in the **Animation** group.

4. Go to the **Motion Paths** area and select the motion path that you would like to use.
5. To get the clip art to move in the direction you would like, *click and drag* the red arrow at the end of the motion path. Make sure that the mouse turns to two-arrows not four arrows. The four-arrow mouse will move the complete motion path.
6. Also check the **Start** status in the **Timing** group (under the **Animations** tab). If you want the clip art to move once the screen is presented, change the **Start – On Click** to **Start – With Previous**.

Clip Art can be altered like pictures. Except GIF images cannot be cropped.

☑Tip: Changing a Clip Art for your special needs.

You can take a WMF clip art and make it your very own special clip art. Find several clip arts that have sections or parts that you would like to use or combined with other clip art parts. Then break up the WMF clip art.

1 Select the clip art go to the **Group** button in the **Picture Tools – Format** tab, in the **Arrange** group.

2 *Click* on the drop down arrow next to **Group** and *click* on **Ungroup**.

3 A Microsoft PowerPoint dialog window will open asking you if you would like to change the clip art to a Microsoft Office drawing object.

4 *Click* **Yes**. Now the clip art is broken into sections, although you can not see the separated sections.

5 To see all the separated sections, you need to **Ungroup** the clip art again.

6 *Click* on the sections that you do not want.

7 Push the **delete** key to remove the unwanted part.

8 *Click* on a part that you want to change color.

9 Under the **Drawing – Format** tab, *click* on the down arrow next to **Shape Fill** in the **Shape Styles** group.

10 Select the color you would like.

11 Continue to do steps 8 through 10, until you have all the parts the color you would like.

12 Move each of the sections from the clip arts you selected to the position you would like them.

13 *Click and drag* the mouse curser over all the desired parts to select all the parts. Or *Shift and click* each part until all the parts are selected.

14 Under **Drawing – Format** tab, *click* **Group** and then *click* on **Group** from the drop down menu.

15 Now you have a special designed WMF clip art.

Chapter 6 Shapes

One of the neat things in PowerPoint 2010 is that not only can you add shapes, but now you can change the shape of some shapes that you add to your presentation.

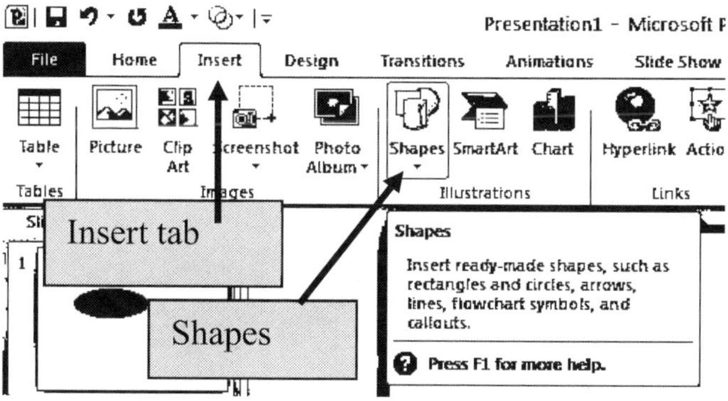

To add shapes to the presentation do the following:

1. *Click* on **Insert**
2. *Click* on **Shapes**
3. Select the shape and then *click and drag* your mouse to draw the shape, this will add it to the presentation.
4. Now *click* on the shape to select it. By clicking on the shape you should have a special menu at the top of the tool bar called **Drawing Tools**.
5. *Click* on the **Drawing Tools - Format** tab. Under the tab, in the **Insert Shapes** group, should be an **Edit Shape** drop down menu, *click* on the down arrow.

6. *Click* on **Edit Points**. The shape now has black end points.
7. *Click* on one of the black end points and two new white points appear.
8. *Click* on one of the white points and drag in or out to change the shape.

Not all shapes can be altered. If the Edit Points command is light or faded out, the command is not available for this shape.

The Combine Add-in

Before you can combine two shapes together you first need to add the **Combine Add-In**. After this Add-in is in PowerPoint you can combine shapes together to get unique shapes. The only problem that I have with combining shapes together is that all the shapes will change to the same color. It would be nice if Microsoft let you change each shape to a unique color. To add the **Combine Shapes** to the **Quick Access** menu follow these steps:

1. *Click* on **File**.
2. Select **Options**.
3. *Click* on **Quick Access Toolbar**. Under the **Choose command from:** - Dropdown menu choose **All Commands.**
4. Go down and select **Combine Shapes**.
5. *Click* **Add** in the middle of the page, and then *click* **OK**. Now the Combine Shape tool is in the **Quick Access** tool bar at the top of the page.

Combining Shapes

To combine two or more shapes do the following steps. One warning is that once the shapes are combined they are treated as one shape, with size, color and movement.

1. *Click* on the **Insert** tab.
2. *Click* on the **Shapes** tab.
3. *Click* on the shape to select it, and then *click* on the presentation page where you want the shape. *Click and drag* your mouse to draw the shape.
4. Repeat the above steps until you have all the shapes that you want to combine.
5. *Click* on all the shapes that you want to combine, by clicking on the first shape and then *Ctrl (control) Click* the other shapes. You can also use the *Shift* key to select all the shapes.
6. *Click* the **Combine Shapes** tool in the **Quick Access** tool bar. A drop down menu appears.
7. Select **Shapes Combine**. Now the shapes are combined to form one shape.
8. You can also select **Shape Union, Shape Intersect**, or **Shape Subtract**.

The color and the shape can be changed using the instructions above.

In PowerPoint editions from 2003 through 2010, logos can be designed outside of PowerPoint on software such as Photoshop or any other graphic package. As long as the picture is saved in an acceptable format for PowerPoint it can be inserted under the Insert tab. Logos now can be designed in PowerPoint 2010 by inserting several designs and then combining them. Additional altering to the shape can be done with the **Edit Shapes – Edit Points** command. To use the **Edit Shapes – Edit Points** tool follow these steps:

1. *Click* on the combined shapes.
2. *Click* on **Drawing Tools – Format** tab.
3. In the **Insert Shapes** group, *click* on **Edit Shape**. A drop down menu appears.
4. *Click* on **Edit Points**. The shape now has black end points.
5. *Click* on one of the black end points and two new white points appear.
6. *Click* on one of the white points and drag in or out to change the shape.

Combining shapes and grouping shapes is not the same thing. When you combine shapes they become one shape. When you group shapes they are still different shapes. They are just grouped together for easy adjustments. One of the problems with combining shapes is that all the combined shapes now take one the same characteristics. The borders are the same and the color is the same. If you would like the shapes to have different colors or different borders, or even animate separately, it might be better to have different shapes grouped together.

Group or Ungroup Shapes

The process for Group or ungroup is the same for shapes, pictures, or other objects. The special **Format** tab will change depending on what you are trying to group. If you are trying to group shapes the special **Format** tab will be **Drawing Tools**. If it is pictures that you are trying to group the special **Format** tab will be **Picture Tools**. It depends on the **Object** that you are trying to group. If you try to group different types of **Objects** then you might have both the **Picture Tools** and the **Drawing Tools** special **Format** tab. You can group shapes, pictures, or other objects. Grouping lets you rotate, flip, move, or resize all shapes or objects at the same time as though they were a single item. You can also change the attributes of all of the items in a group at one time. For example you can change an effect or color. You can select an item within a group and apply an attribute without ungrouping the shapes, or you can create groups within groups to help you build complex drawings.

To group pictures, shapes or objects together follow these steps:

1. *Click* on a shape.
2. *Control (Ctrl) click* the second picture or shape. *Control (Ctrl) click* any other item that you would like to add to the group. (Hold *CTRL and click* on the shapes or other objects that you want to group. You can also use the *Shift* key while you *click* on the shapes or objects.)
3. *Click* on the **Drawing Tools - Format** tab.
4. In the **Arrange** group, *click* on the **Group** drop down arrow, and then *click* **Group**.

If you do not see the **Drawing Tools - Format** tabs, make sure that you selected a shape or other object. You might have to *double-click* the object to open the **Format** tab.

Now you can make your changes. Move, change color or add effects. After you group pictures or other objects, you can continue to select any single picture or object within the group. Select the group, and then *click* the individual picture or object that you want to select.

You can also ungroup a group of shapes at any time and then regroup them later.

Once you have grouped shapes, pictures or objects together it is easy to save them as a picture for future use. *Right – click* on the grouped items and select **Save as Picture**. Give the new picture and name and save it.

Ungroup shapes

To ungroup a group of shapes, pictures, or other objects (for example, if you want to move a group but leave one shape behind or make extensive changes to one shape without changing the other shapes), do the following:

1. Select the group that you want to ungroup.
2. *Click* on **Drawing Tools - Format** tab, in the **Arrange** group.
3. *Click* on **Group** dropdown arrow.
4. *Click* **Ungroup**.

If you do not see the **Drawing Tools**, **Picture Tools**, or **Format** tabs, make sure that you selected a group of shapes, pictures, or other objects. You might have to *double-click* the object to open the **Format** tab.

Regroup shapes

To select anyone of the pictures or objects that was previously in a group do the following:

1. Select any one of the shapes or objects that were previously in a group.
2. Select **Drawing Tools - Format** tab.
3. In the **Arrange** group, *click* **Group**.
4. *Click* **Regroup**.

If you do not see the **Drawing Tools** or **Format** tabs, make sure that you selected a picture or other object. You might have to *double-click* the object to open the **Format** tab.

Changing Colors of Shapes

Once you have added a shape to the page you can change the color of the shape or the outline of the shape.

1. *Click* on the shape.
2. *Click* on **Drawing Tools – Format** tab.
3. Under the **Shape Styles** group do one of the following:
    a. *Click* on the **More** drop down arrow in the lower right hand corner of the shape styles examples. The window opens to selections of outlined, filled or accented options. Select the option that you like.
    b. *Click* on **Fill** and choose one of the following options:
        i. **No Fill**. If you don't want the shape to be filled. Make sure that you have selected a border otherwise the shape disappears.
        ii. **Solid Fill**. *Click* on the drop down arrow next to the **Color** box. *Click* on a color you like.
        iii. **Gradient Fill.** *Click* on the **Gradient stops** and select a color gradient you like. You can add or remove the colors with the buttons on the right of the gradient slide bar.

iv. **Picture of Texture Fill**. Select a picture by *clicking* on the **Insert From** boxes. If you selected **Insert From: File**, the **Insert Picture** dialog window opens. *Click* on a picture, and *click* **Insert**. If you want a texture click on the drop down box next to **Texture**. Select the texture you want.

v. **Pattern Fill**. Select a pattern.

vi. **Slide Background Fill**. This gives the effect of a hole. So the background shows through. If you have a shape that you want to put a hole in, so the background shows, this is a great tool.

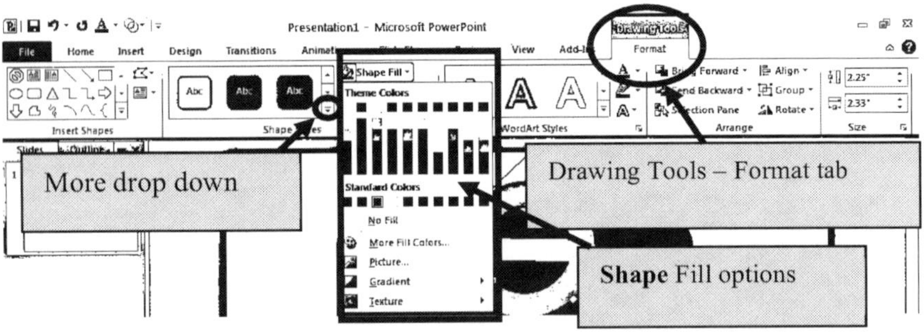

Under **Gradient and Texture** you also have the option to select **More Gradient** or **More Texture**, which will open the **Format Shape** dialog window. In the **Format Shape** dialog window you have many more options to alter the shape and change the color.

☑**Tip: Getting the color just right** (Repeat Tip)

When you need to get the color as close as possible, you may need to use a third party software to find the RGB color numbers. The RGB numbers range from 0 to 255 for each color (Red, Green and Blue). Most third party software use a dropper or magnifying class icon to find the RGB numbers, that you click on and then move your mouse over the color that you are trying to find the RGB for, the software will calculate the RBG numbers. Just copy these RGB numbers into the **More Fill Colors** dialog box, under the **Custom** tab.

I use a free third party color finder called Color Cop (http://www.colorcop.net). The owner of the site asks for a donation. I have found this software easy to use and pretty accurate. You do have to remember that the color of your slides will change from screen to screen and change even more when using projectors.

Adding Borders to Shapes

You can add borders to any shape, and then you can change the color of the border.

1. *Click* on the shape that you want to add a border.
2. *Click* on **Drawing Tools – Format** tab.
3. Under the **Shape Styles** group, *click* on **Shape Outline.**
4. *Click* on the color that you would like the border to be.
5. *Click* on **Shape Outline** again. Go down to **Weight**.
6. *Click* on the weight of the border you would like.
7. Now the shape has a border in the selected color.

Changing Shapes

If you added a shape to the page and decided that you would like to have a different shape, you could delete the shape and add a new shape. But what if you already changed the border, changed to color and may be you have a lot of time already involved in getting the shape like you want it, just a different shape would be better. Or you copied a shape because you liked the color and effects but now the new shape needs to be changed. This is easily done in PowerPoint.

1. *Click* on the shape that you would like to be replaced.
2. *Click* on **Drawing Tools – Format** tab.
3. Under the **Insert Shapes** group, *click* on **Edit Shape.**
4. Select **Change Shape**.
5. *Click* on the shape that you would like to use.
6. The old shape changes to the new shape.

☑Tip: Changing the Shape of the Shape

This is so cool; in PowerPoint 2010 you can change the shape of shapes to make your own unique shape. You can also change text boxes into shapes and then change the text boxes shape. This tool is not available for all shapes and sometimes you have to change a text box to a rectangle before you can change the shape of the text box. Once you have added a shape to the page you can reshape the outline of the shape by following these steps.

1. *Click* on the shape.
2. *Click* on **Drawing Tools – Format** tab.
3. Under the **Insert Shapes** group, *click* on **Edit Shape.**

4. *Click* on **Edit Points**. If the **Edit Points** option is not available, then you have to **Change Shape** first. **Change Shape** option requires that you select a shape that can be altered.
5. After *clicking* **Edit Shape**, the shape will have small black boxes on the edge of the shape. When you move the mouse over one of the black boxes it will change to a black-outlined box with four arrows pointing outward from the sides. Sometimes you may get white boxes with a black-outline.
6. *Click* on the black box, now there should be two blue lines extruding from the black-outlined box. You can do any of the following:
    a. *Click and drag* the center black-outlined box, and the shape will change.
    b. *Click* on one of the outer white boxes and *click and drag*, the shape will change. By *clicking* on the outer white boxes you change the shape of the lines on either side of the center box.

Adding Text to Shapes

Text can be added to shapes, even if you have filled the shape with a picture. But a picture cannot have text. On a picture you have to add a text box or WordArt above the picture. If you added a picture to the shape or you have a shape with a texture, filled color or a transparent fill you can add text just by clicking on the shape and start typing. To add text to a shape, *click* the shape and start typing.

Aligning Text on Shapes

Sometimes when you add text to a shape it is not aligned where you would like it to be. Different shapes align text differently. Therefore it is important to change the alignment to have a special look. If the text in the shape cannot be aligned just right you may have to use a Text Box or WordArt and position them on top of the shape. To align the words within the shape do the following:

1. Highlight the word (text), and *click* on the **Home** tab.
2. Under the **Paragraph** group, you can:

- Bullet or number the text lists.
- Decrease or Increase the list level.
- Increase or decrease line spacing
- Align text left, center, right, justified or distribute the text.
- Split the text into columns.
- Change the orientation of the text. Under **Text Direction** you can *click* on **More Options** and the **Format Text Effects** window will open. *Click* on **Text Box**. Here you can alter the location of the text in more detail.
- Align text to the top, middle, or bottom of the shape.
- Convert the test to **SmartArt**.

If the text is still not fitting to your requirements you can go to the Font group, where you can:

- Change the type of fonts.

- Change the size of the fonts.
- Bold, italic, or underline the text.
- Shadow the text.
- Strikethrough the text.
- Space out the characters.
- Change case of the text.
- Increase or decrease the fonts by *clicking* on the large **A** or small **A**.
- Change the text color.
- Or Clear all formatting.

☑**Tip: Text box insert on top of a shape.**

When you rotate shapes the text in the shape also rotates. This can be a problem if you want straight text with a rotated shape. A nice part about using WordArt or a separate text box over a shape is that you can rotate the text separate from the shape. By using separate shapes and text box you can rotate either one and get the exact design you want. If the text is part of the shape you can rotate them together, but you can't keep the shape straight and rotate the text to fit, or vise-versa.

Rotating Shapes

You can rotate shapes, object, text boxes and WordArt. You rotate by moving your mouse over the green dot above the shape, object, text box or WordArt, and when the mouse arrow turns to a round arrow *click and drag* to the angle that you would like.

Animating Shapes

Shapes are one of the most animated objects in PowerPoint, probably right behind text. Note: Too much animation can actually hurt your presentation delivery causing you to distract audiences away from your message.

1. *Click* on the shape.
2. *Click* the **Animations** tab.
3. In the **Animation** group, select the type of animation you would like.
4. For additional animation effects *click* the drop down arrow on the right side of the animation example. Animations are broken into groups of entrances, emphasis, exits and motion paths. Note that entrance animations are in green, emphasis animations are in yellow and exit animations are in red.
5. *Click* the animation you would like. If the shape is visible, once the mouse is hovering over the animation the shape will play the animation, showing the animation of the shape.

Set the animation effect options

To set the animation effect options, do the following:

1. Select the animated shape that you want to modify.
2. *Click* the **Animations** tab. Under the **Animations** group, c*lick* the **Effect Options** button that is to the right of the animation examples.
3. A drop down list appears that give you option for the particular animation you have chosen. For example if you had a **Wipe** animation the **Effect**

Options might give you the option to wipe from the bottom, wipe from the left, wipe from the right or wipe from the top.

Another way to change the effects of an animated shape is to open the **Animation Pane**. To change the effects in the **Animation Pane** do the following.

1. *Click* on the animated shape.
2. *Click* on the **Animations** tab.
3. *Click* **Animation Pane** under the **Advanced Animation** group.
4. In the **Animation Pane** list, *click* the drop down arrow to the right of the animation that you want to modify.
5. Select **Effect Options**.
6. In the dialog box, on the **Effect** tab, in the **Settings** group, *click* the **Direction** drop down box.
7. Select the effect option you would like.

Animation Painter

One of the new features in Microsoft PowerPoint 2010 is the Animation Painter. Using the Animation Painter, you can easily and quickly copy an animation or several animations from one object to another.

To copy animations from one object to another, do the following:

1. Select the object (picture, shape or text) with the animations that you want to copy.
2. *Click* on the **Animations** tab.

3. In the **Advanced Animation** group, *click* **Animation Painter**.
4. *Click* the chart that you want to copy the animations onto.
5. The animation is now copied to the new object.

Remove Animations

1. *Click* on the shape with the animation that you want to remove.
2. *Click* on the **Animations** tab.
3. In the **Animation** group *click* **None**. If you don't see **None**, *click* the drop down arrow on the right side of the animation example for more options. **None** is mostly the top option.

Timing or Effect Options

You can customize the timing of animation effects in Microsoft PowerPoint 2010, including the timing and order with which they start, and whether they repeat.

To set the start time for an animation effect, follow these steps:

1. *Click* on the shape that you want to set the timing.
2. *Click* on the **Animations** tab.
3. In the **Timing** group, do one of the following:

- To start the animation effect when you *click* the slide, select **Start:** On Click
- To start the animation effect at the same time as the previous effect in the list (one click executes multiple animation effects), select **Start:** With Previous

- To start the animation effect immediately after the previous effect in the list finishes playing (you do not have to click again to make the next animation effect start), select **Start:** After Previous

Duration of / or Delaying Animations

1. *Click* on the shape that contains the animation effect for which you want to set a delay or other timing option.
2. *Click* on the **Animations** tab.
3. In the **Timing** group, do one or more of the following:

- To specify the length of an animation effect, enter a number in the **Duration** box.
- To create a delay between the end of one animation effect and the start of a new animation effect, enter a number in the **Delay** box.

Repeat or Rewind an Animation Effect

You can make an animation repeat a number of times (2, 3, 4, 5, or 10 times), **Until Next Click**, or **Until End of Slide**. To make an animation effect or sequence of effects repeat or return to its original position, follow these steps:

1. *Click* on the shape that you want the animation to repeat.
2. *Click* on the **Animations** tab.
3. In the **Animation** group, *click* on the arrow in the lower right-hand corner of the Animation group

box. This is called **Show Additional Effect Options** launcher.

4. A new window appears, *click* the **Timing** tab, and then do one or more of the following:

- To select a repeat option *click* on the **Repeat** drop down arrow, and select an option in the **Repeat** list.
- To automatically return an animation effect to its original look and location after it plays, select the **Rewind When Done Playing** check box.

Changing Animation Order

Animated objects on a slide display a number indicating the order in which the object's animation plays. When there are two or more animation effects, you can change the order in which each plays by doing one of the following:

- On the slide, *click* an animation that you want to move up or down in the sequence, and then on the **Animations** tab, in the **Timing** group, under **Reorder Animation**, click **Move Earlier** or **Move Later**.
- On the **Animations** tab, in the **Advanced Animation** group, *click* **Animation Pane**. You can change the order by *clicking and dragging* objects up or down in the list, or *click* on the item you want to move and then use the **Re-Order** arrows at the bottom of the **Animation Pane**. You can also *click* an object in the **Animation Pane** and then in the

Timing group, under **Reorder Animation**, *click* **Move Earlier** or **Move Later**.

Trigger an Animation

With triggers, you can make an animation effect occur during a slide show when you *click* an object on the slide or when you play a specific part of a video.

Set a trigger on click

1. Select the object that has the animation that you want to trigger.
2. *Click* on the **Animations** tab.
3. In the **Advanced Animation** group, *click* **Trigger**.
4. *Click* **On Click of**, and select the object that you want to trigger the animation.

Disable Animations

1. *Click* on the **Slide Show** tab.
2. Under the **Set Up** group, *click* **Set Up Slide Show**.
3. In the **Set Up Show** dialog box, under **Show options**, select the **Show without animation** check box.
4. *Click* **OK**.

Chapter 7 SmartArt

SmartArt is a great way to add organization charts, flow charts and many other dynamic charts that add to your presentation.

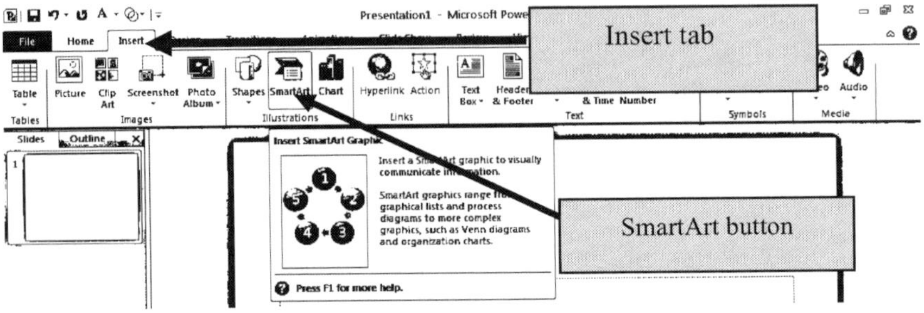

To add a SmartArt to your presentation do the following:

1. *Click* on the **Insert** tab
2. *Click* on **SmartArt**
3. A full array of charts will display in the **Choose a SmartArt Graphic** window. The list is broken down by chart type or you can select **All** and a full list is displayed. Use the slider to move down to see other charts.
4. *Click* on the chart you would like
5. The chart is displayed to the right of the list.
6. If you like the chart *click* **OK**.

Resize SmartArt

To resize the SmartArt do the following:

1. Move the mouse to a corner. The courser will change to a double arrow line.

2. *Click and drag* the corner in or out to resize. This can also be done at any location on the **SmartArt** where dots appear along the edge.

Show the Text Box of a SmartArt

On the left edge of the SmartArt is an extruding double arrow rectangle. *Click* on this rectangle and the text box appears. Text can be added either here or on the SmartArt where [Text] is indicated. To close the text box use the **X** in the upper right hand corner.

Changing Color of SmartArt

To change the color of the SmartArt, follow these steps:

1. *Click* on the **SmartArt**
2. A special **SmartArt Tools** tab is present on the ribbon. *Click* on the **Design** tab under the **SmartArt Tools** tab.
3. *Click* on **Change Colors** under the **SmartArt Styles** group. A new window will appear. The options let you change colors of the **SmartArt** or change color of each section of the **SmartArt**. When you move your mouse over the color section the **SmartArt** on the slide will change color to show the results. These colors should match the Theme, so if you change Themes the colors will change.
4. *Click* on the one you would like to use
5. The **SmartArt** on the slide has changed.

Change color of an individual part of the SmartArt

To change a color of one section of the SmartArt, do the following:

1. *Click* on the part of the **SmartArt** that you want to change. There will now be dots around the selected piece only. You may have to *double-click* the individual part to select it.
2. The special **SmartArt Tools** tab is visible on the ribbon. *Click* on **Format** under the **SmartArt Tools** tab.
3. *Click* on the down arrow next to **Shape Fill** in the **Shape Styles** group.
4. Select the color that you would like and *click* on it.
5. The color on the selected part of the SmartArt has changed.

Changing the Location of SmartArt

You can move the SmartArt by moving the mouse to the edge of the SmartArt, when the mouse arrow changes to a four-arrow curser you can *click and drag* the SmartArt.

If you want to move just part of the SmartArt follow these steps:

1. *Click* on the section you want to move. If you want to move several sections use the *Shift-Click* or *Ctrl-Click* commands to select those sections.
2. To move those sections:
    a. Move the mouse over them until the mouse curser becomes four-arrows.

b. *Click and drag* to the location you would like.

3. To rotate sections of the SmartArt:
   a. Move the mouse over the green dot that may be above the section or to the side of the section. The curser will become a circle.
   b. *Click* and move right or left to move the section.

Grouping and Ungrouping SmartArt

Ungroup SmartArt

SmartArt sections are grouped together. All the shapes within the SmartArt are grouped within the perimeter of the SmartArt. You cannot move a shape out of the perimeter, unless you ungroup the SmartArt.

To **Ungroup** a SmartArt object (for example, if you want to move a section of the SmartArt away from the other parts of the SmartArt or to make changes to the separate section but leave the other sections in tack and unchanged), do the following:

1. Select the SmartArt that you want to ungroup.
2. Under **SmartArt Tools - Format** tab, in the **Arrange** group, *click* **Group.** If the word **Group** is not visible, select the double box icon to the right of Send Backward.
3. *Click* **Ungroup**. Now ever item of the SmartArt is a separate section. Now you can change the location, angle or shape of the one of the sections.

Re-Group or Group SmartArt

To re-group the sections of a SmartArt, first *click* on one of the sections then follow these steps:

1. *Click* on the **Drawing Tools – Format** tab.
2. *Click* on **Group** in the drop down box.
3. *Click* on **Regroup** or **Group**.

SmartArt can also be grouped with other objects such as pictures, or text. To group these items together *Shift-click or Ctrl click* the items and then go to **Drawing Tools – Format** tab and under **Group** *click* **Group**. The problem with ungrouping the SmartArt is that the ungrouped shapes cannot be converted back to SmartArt.

Changing Shapes within SmartArt

You can change the shape of a section of the SmartArt. Follow these steps change the shape of SmartArt:

1. *Click* on the selected section within the SmartArt.
2. Under **Drawing Tools – Format**, *click* **Change Shape** in the **Shapes** group.
3. The shape example dialog window opens. Select the shape that you would like to insert.

☑Tip: Changing SmartArt to Shapes or Text.

There are times when the SmartArt is unable to give you the look you want. You may have to change the SmartArt into shapes so you can move them or give them a unique look. This is done through the **Convert** tab.

1. *Click* on the **SmartArt**.
2. *Click* on **SmartArt Tools – Design** tab.
3. In the **Reset** group *click* on **Convert**.

4. Select either **Convert to Text** or **Convert to Shapes.**

Animating SmartArt

You can create moving, animated SmartArt graphics to provide additional emphasis or show your information in phases. You can animate your entire SmartArt graphic or only an individual shape in your SmartArt graphic.

Animations for SmartArt graphics

Animations that you apply to a SmartArt graphic are different from animations that you can apply to shapes, text, or WordArt in the following ways:

- The connecting lines between shapes in SmartArt are always associated with the second shape and are not animated individually.
- If you apply an animation to shapes in a SmartArt graphic, the animation plays in the order that the shapes appear. The order can be reversed only as a whole. Thus, you cannot reorder the sequence of animations for a single SmartArt graphic (besides reversing the order that the shapes appear).

Example: If you have six shapes and each contains a single letter A through F, you can play the animation from A to F or F to A. You cannot play the animation out of order, such as A to C and then F to D. However, you can create multiple slides to mimic this order. In this example, you can create one slide that animates shapes A to C and a second slide that animates shapes F to D.

Add an animation

Not all animation effects can be used with SmartArt, some animation effects that will not work with SmartArt are **Drop, Flip** or **Whip**. Effects that are unavailable for SmartArt graphics will appear dimmed.

To use the animation effects that are unavailable for SmartArt graphics, do the following:

1. *Right-click* the SmartArt graphic.
2. *Click* **Convert to Shapes.**
3. And then animate the shapes.

How to Animate SmartArt

1. *Click* the SmartArt graphic.
2. *Click* the **Animations** tab.
3. In the **Animation** group *click* the animation that you would like.
4. For Additional animation effects *click* the drop down arrow on the right side of the animation examples. Animations are broken into groups of entrances, emphasis, exits and motion paths. Note that entrance animations are in green, emphasis animations are in yellow and exit animations are in red.
5. The whole SmartArt will move together.

Set the animation effect options

To set the animation effect options, do the following:

1. Select the animated SmartArt that you want to modify.
2. *Click* the **Animations** tab.
3. In the **Animations** group, c*lick* the **Effect Options** button that is to the right of the animation examples. This option will only change the effect for the whole SmartArt. *Click* on the option that you want.

Or do the following under the **Advanced Animation** group.

1. C*lick* **Animation Pane**. This option gives you more flexibility with your animation and lets individual parts move separately from the rest of the SmartArt.
2. In the **Animation Pane** list, *click* the drop down arrow to the right of the animation that you want to modify.
3. Select **Effect Options**.
4. In the dialog box, on the **SmartArt Animation** tab, in the **Group graphic** list, select one of the following options: (Not all these options are available with every SmartArt.)

- **As One Object -** The animation is applied as if the whole SmartArt graphic as one picture or object. The SmartArt all moves together, as if they are one object.
- **All at Once -** All of the shapes in the SmartArt graphic are animated at the same time. But there

is movement within the SmartArt during the animation. Each shape moves independent of the others, but arrive at their destination at the same time. Different animations move differently, with some SmartArt the animation difference between **As One Object** and **All at Once** maybe minute.

- **One by One -** Each shape is animated individually, one after the other.
- **By Level at Once -** All shapes at the same level are animated at the same time. If text is on a layer above the shapes, the shapes will all move at the same time, and then the text will move. Sometimes a shape and a text are on the same level and will move at the same time. SmartArt graphics have different levels with some having all the shapes on one level and others have the shapes on different levels. To view the sequence of the movement, click on the double drop down arrows below and to the left of the Diagram in the Animation Pane. The list of animations is shown in the order in which they occur, and cannot be changed.
- **By Level One by One –** Each text and shape if located in a different level will be animated at different times. The SmartArt graphics are animated first by level and then individually within that level, and is hard to predict which level will animate first. Some SmartArt will have the text move first while others have the shape move first.

Caution should be taken when using this option to make sure the order of the animation is exactly what you want. To view the sequence of the movement, click on the double drop down arrows below and to the left of the Diagram in the Animation Pane. The list of animations is shown in the order in which they occur, and can not be changed.

Animation Painter

One of the new features in Microsoft PowerPoint 2010 is the Animation Painter. Using the Animation Painter, you can easily and quickly copy an animation or several animations from one SmartArt graphic to another.

To copy animations from one SmartArt graphic to another, do the following:

1. Select the SmartArt graphic with the animations that you want to copy.
2. On the **Animations** tab, in the **Advanced Animation** group, *click* **Animation Painter**.
3. *Click* the SmartArt graphic that you want to copy the animations onto.

Removing Animations

If there is a shape that you do not want to animate you can remove the animation from that shape as long as you animated the SmartArt with any of the options other than **As One Object.** As long as the SmartArt animation shows the double drop down arrows in the **Animation**

Pane window, you can remove the animation from any of the detailed movements.

1. *Click* the SmartArt graphic that you want to remove an animation.
2. *Click* the **Animation** tab.
3. *Click* on the **Animation Pane** tab, under the **Advanced Animation** group.
4. In the **Animation Pane**, *click* on the down arrow or double down arrows if you have more than one animation, to open up the individual animations.
5. If you have more than one animation *click* on the Animation you want to remove. This can be very hard to determine, you will have to know the order in which the shapes are animated, because the names given in the **Animation Pane** do not identify any one particular shape.
6. *Click* on the right drop down arrow.
7. *Click* on **Remove**. If you only have one animation you can skip steps 5 & 6.

Be careful when removing an animation on a shape in SmartArt. You cannot just add the animation back. To add the animation back to the shape you will have to redo the animation for the complete SmartArt. You can also remove multiple, specific animation effects. *Press and hold CTRL*, and then in the **Animation Task** pane, select each animation effect that you want to remove, *right-click* one of the selected effects and select **Remove**.

Reverse the Order of Animations

1. *Click* the SmartArt graphic with the animation that you want to reverse.

2. On the **Animations** tab, in the **Advanced Animation** group, *click* **Animation Pane**.
3. Select the animation that you want to reverse.
4. *Click* on the drop down arrow next to the animated diagram.
5. *Click* **Effect Options**.
6. *Click* the **SmartArt Animation** tab.
7. Check the box next to **Reverse order**.

Remove an animation from the SmartArt

1. *Click* the SmartArt graphic with the animation that you want to remove.
2. On the **Animations** tab, in the **Animation** group *click* **None**. If you don't see **None**, *click* the drop down arrow on the right side of the animation example for more options. **None** is mostly the top option.

Animation Timing or Effect Options

You can customize the timing of animation effects in Microsoft PowerPoint 2010, including the timing and order with which they start, and whether they repeat.

To set the start time for an animation effect, follow these steps:

1. *Click* on the SmartArt that you want to set the timing.
2. On the **Animations** tab, in the **Timing** group, do one of the following:

a. To start the animation effect when you *click* the slide, select **Start:** On Click

b. To start the animation effect at the same time as the previous effect in the list (that is, one *click* executes multiple animation effects), select **Start:** With Previous

c. To start the animation effect immediately after the previous effect in the list finishes playing (that is, you do not have to *click* again to make the next animation effect start), select **Start:** After Previous

Duration or Delaying Animations

1. *Click* on the SmartArt that contains the animation effect for which you want to set a delay or other timing option.
2. On the **Animations** tab, in the **Timing** group, do one or more of the following:

- To specify the length of an animation effect, enter a number in the **Duration** box.
- To create a delay between the end of one animation effect and the start of a new animation effect, enter a number in the **Delay** box.

Repeat or rewind an animation effect

You can make an animation repeat a number of times (2, 3, 4, 5, or 10 times), **Until Next Click**, or **Until End of Slide**. To make an animation effect or sequence of effects repeat or return to its original position, follow these steps:

1. *Click* on the SmartArt that you want to repeat.
2. On the **Animations** tab, in the **Animation** group, *click* on the arrow in the lower right-hand corner of the **Animation** group box. This is called **Show Additional Effect Options** launcher.
3. A new window appears, *click* the **Timing** tab, and then do one or more of the following:
    a. To select a repeat option click on the **Repeat** drop down arrow, and select an option in the **Repeat** list.
    b. To automatically return an animation effect to its original look and location after it plays, select the **Rewind when done playing** check box. In some cases this will make the SmartArt disappear after the animation.

Animation Order

Animated objects on a slide display a number indicating the order in which the object's animation plays. When there are two or more animation effects, you can change the order in which each plays by doing one of the following:

- On the slide, *click* an animation that you want to move up or down in the sequence, and then on the **Animations** tab, in the **Timing** group, under **Reorder Animation**, *click* **Move Earlier** or **Move Later**.
- On the **Animations** tab, in the **Advanced Animation** group, *click* **Animation Pane**. You can

change the order by *dragging* objects up or down in the list.

- Or you can *click* on the item you want to move and then use the **Re-Order** arrows at the bottom of the **Animation Pane**. You can also *click* an object in the **Animation Pane** and then in the **Timing** group, under **Reorder Animation**, *click* **Move Earlier** or **Move Later**.

Note: Some animations in SmartArt cannot be **Re-Ordered** or **Moved**. Some animations orders in SmartArt are set in stone. Sometimes this can be changed if you set the animations effect options to another setting.

Trigger an Animation

With triggers, you can make an animation effect occur during a slide show when you *click* an object on the slide or when you play a specific part of a video. This will not work if you only have one SmartArt on the slide.

Set a Trigger on Click

1. Select the object that has the animation that you want to trigger.
2. On the **Animations** tab, in the **Advanced Animation** group, *click* **Trigger**.
3. *Click* **On Click of**, and select the object that you want to trigger the animation.

Or you can do the following (either way will work)

1. On the **Animations** tab, in the **Advanced Animation** group, *click* **Animation Pane** to open the **Animation Pane.**

2. In the **Animation Pane**, select the animation that you want to trigger.
3. In the **Advanced Animation** group, *click* **Trigger**, point to **On Click** of, and select the object that you want to trigger the animation.

Disable animations from playing in Slide Show view

1. *Click* on the **Slide Show** tab.
2. Under the **Set Up** group, *click* **Set Up Slide Show**.
3. In the **Set Up Show** dialog box, under **Show Options**, select the **Show Without Animation** check box.
4. *Click* **OK**.

Chapter 8 Charts

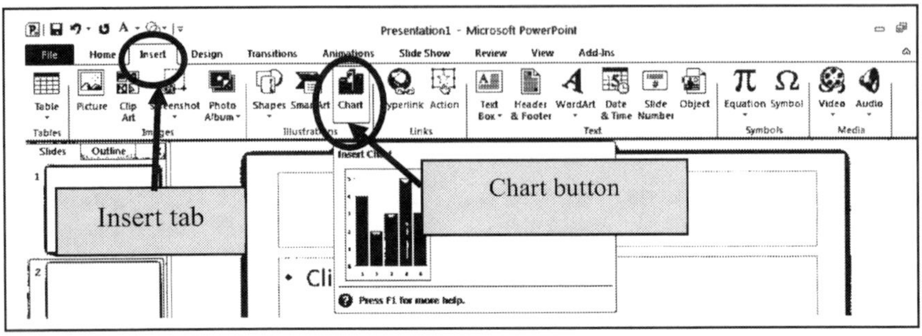

Charts that are inserted in PowerPoint are connected to **PowerPoint - Excel** worksheets not true **Excel** worksheets like we have been taught to believe. Let me explain. If you make a chart in PowerPoint an Excel worksheet opens up with sample data.

Change the data and save the data as an Excel worksheet, giving the new worksheet a new name. Now look at name of the worksheet on the top of the Excel worksheet. The name did not change.

Close the worksheet and go back to the chart in PowerPoint. *Click* on the chart then *click* on **Edit Data** in the **Data** group under the **Chart Tools – Design** tab. The worksheet is the same Excel worksheet that was opened with the chart, not the one you saved.

The worksheet you saved is not connected to any chart on the PowerPoint slide. That is why it is important to know what is going on with tables and charts in PowerPoint.

There are several ways to add charts to PowerPoint. When you add a table to your presentation, PowerPoint does not let you put a chart with the table, so if you want a chart with a table it is best to insert a chart not a table, and then pick the option to include a table with the chart.

To add an Excel chart to a PowerPoint presentation, go to the **Insert** tab and *click* on **Chart**. In PowerPoint 2010 the chart will open on the presentation, plus the table will open in Excel. In PowerPoint 2010 you can always edit the data by *right clicking* on the chart then select **Edit Data**, this will open the Excel table. Or you can edit the data by using the **Edit Data** button under the **Data** group in the **Chart Tools – Design** tab. As you enter data in the worksheet the chart will update automatically. To close the Excel table use Windows normal procedures.

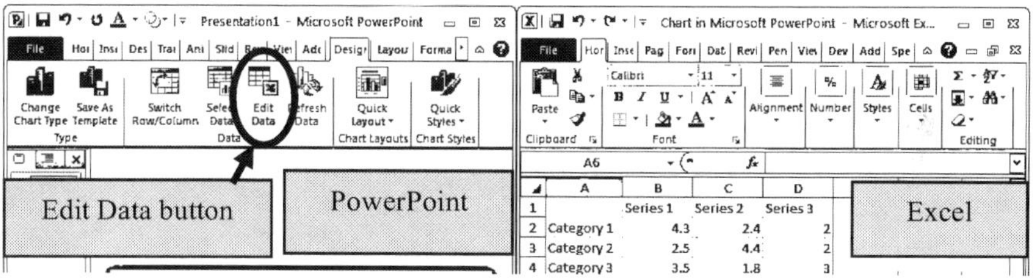

Let's first get started in charts by showing how to insert a chart in the presentation. You can insert a chart two ways. The first and easiest way is to *click* on the chart symbol in the middle of a new slide. This slide layout is a slide option in your master slide setup.

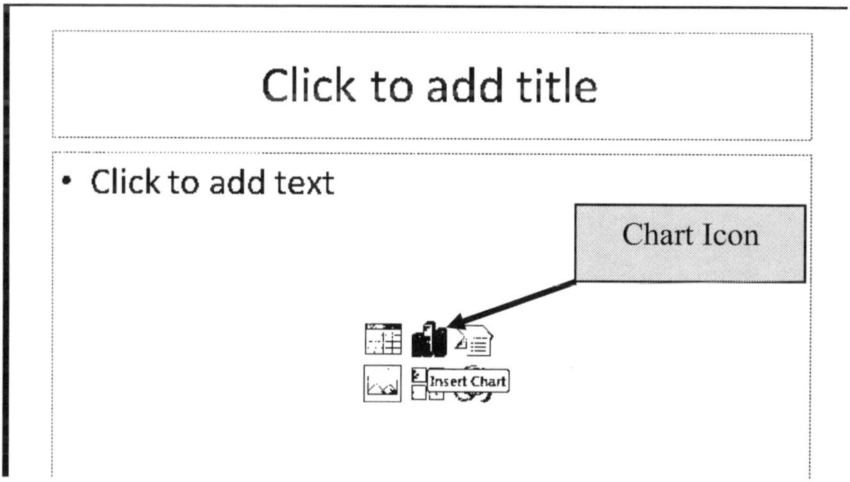

1. *Click* on the Chart Icon.
2. The **Insert Chart** window appears.
3. *Click* on the type of chart you would like.
4. *Click* **OK**.
5. Excel will open with a table that is already populated with row and column headings and data.
6. Rename the row and column headings.
7. Insert new data
8. To increase the table: *click* on the lower right hand corner of the table (there is a blue triangle) and *drag* the table to the size you would like.
9. You can close Excel. The chart is up-dated and the worksheet is saved automatically.

The second way to insert a chart is:

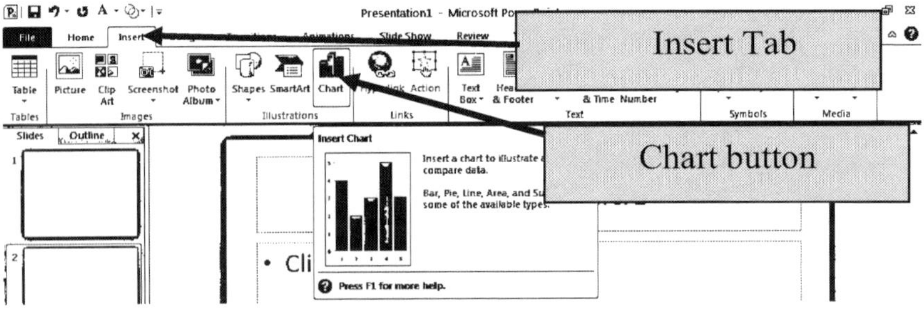

1. *Click* on the **Insert** tab.
2. *Click* on **Chart**.
3. *Click* on the type of chart you would like.
4. *Click* **OK**.
5. Excel will open with a table that is already populated with row and column headings and data.
6. Rename the row and column headings.

7. Insert new data
8. To increase the table: *click* on the lower right hand corner of the table (there is a blue triangle) and drag the table to the size you would like.
9. You can save and close Excel. The chart is up-dated automatically.

When you add a chart to a slide, PowerPoint adds a new tab on the ribbon. The new tab will help you add to the chart or change things in your chart. The new tab is **Chart Tools**, with sub-tabs **Design, Layout**, and **Format** tabs. If you don't see the **Chart Tools**, make sure that you *click* anywhere inside the chart to activate it. You can also access design, layout, and formatting features that are available for specific chart elements (such as chart axes or the legend) by *right-clicking* those chart elements.

Editing Data in Charts

To change the data for the chart do the following:

1. *Click* on the chart.
2. *Click* on **Chart Tools – Design** tab.
3. Under the **Data** group *click* on **Edit Data**.
4. The Excel worksheet will open.
5. Edit the data and close the Excel worksheet.
6. The chart in PowerPoint is automatically up-dated and the worksheet is saved.

Changing the chart

After you create a chart, you can change the way it looks or even the type of chart you want. To avoid a lot of manual formatting, Microsoft Office PowerPoint 2010 provides a variety of useful predefined quick layouts and styles that you may want apply to your chart. You can then customize the chart further by manually changing the layout and formatting style of its individual chart elements.

You can change the appearance of the chart by taking advantage of PowerPoint's chart design tools or by changing individual parts of the chart. PowerPoint charts can be altered like charts in Excel.

To change the chart type, follow these steps:

1. *Click* on the chart you would like to change
2. Under **Chart Tools – Design** *click* on **Change Chart Type** in the **Type** group.
3. A **Change Chart Type** dialog window opens. Select the type of chart you want.
4. *Click* **OK**.

Changing sections of a Chart

If you want to change individual parts of the chart follow these steps.

1. Either *click* or *click* twice on the part of the chart that you want to change. A single *click* might highlight related items. For example, in a bar chart if you click on one of the bars that represents sales data for one year, you might also highlight the bars that represent sales data for the other years in the chart. So you might have to *click twice* just to highlight sales data for just one year. Note: *double-clicking* on a part of the chart might bring up a special dialog window that is related to the part of the chart that you *doubled-clicked* on.

2. *Click* on **Chart Tools – Format**.
3. Under the **Shape Styles** group *click* on **Shape Fill**.
4. Select the color that you want.
5. The selected part of the chart will change color.

Change the whole chart.

1. *Click* once on the chart. Every section of the chart will be highlighted with light-blue dots.
2. *Click* on **Chart Tools – Design**.
3. Under the **Chart Styles** group *click* the color pattern that you like. If you do not see the style that fits your fancy, *click* on the **More** down arrow on the right edge of the **Chart Style** group.
4. *Click* the style you like and the chart changes to that style. The color selection may be limited to the theme of the presentation. To change color options go to **Design** tab (not the **Chart Tools – Design** tab), and *click* on the **Colors** drop down box under the **Themes** group. As you move the mouse over the custom color themes the chart on the presentation page will change.

Titles, Legends, & Axes in Charts

If you would like to design the chart with labels and titles do the following:

1. *Click* on the chart.
2. *Click* on **Chart Tools – Layout**.

- Under the **Layout** tab you can insert pictures, shapes and text to the chart.
- You can add chart titles, axes titles, legends data labels and data tables.
- For certain charts you can also add trend lines, lines, up/down bars, and error bars.

Using predefined chart layouts

If you want to add a table to your chart or you want to change the chart to a PowerPoint chart format, you have some easy predefined charts that look professional and that can be altered to fit your needs. Many times you will find it is easier to find a predefined chart that is close to what you want instead of making all the alterations in the **Chart Tools - Layout** or **Chart Tools - Format** tabs. To change to a predefined chart follow these steps:

1. Select the chart that you want to format.
2. Under **Chart Tools - Design** tab, in the **Chart Layouts** group, *click* on one of the examples or *click* the **More** drop down arrow.
3. *Click* on the chart layout that you want to use.

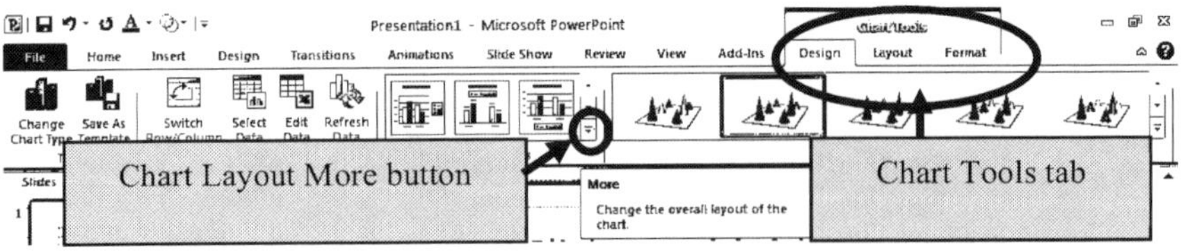

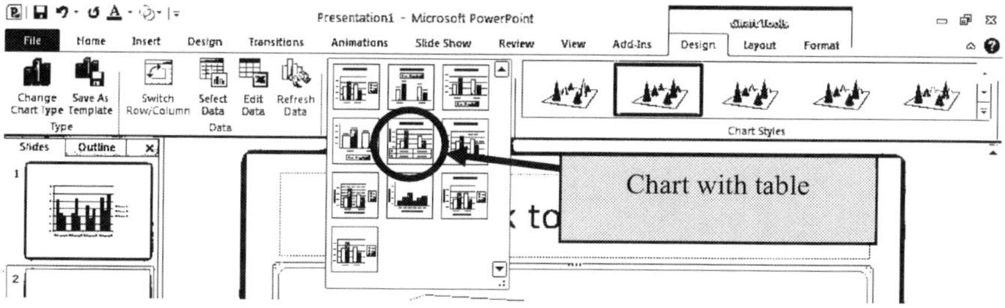

If you don't see **Chart Tools** or the **Design** tab, make sure you have selected a chart.

Colors and Theme Colors within Charts

Chart styles use the colors of the current document theme that is applied to the workbook. You can change the colors by switching to a different theme. You can also customize a chart by following these steps:

1. Select the section of the chart you want to change. You may have to *click twice* on the section you want.
2. *Double click* on the selected area. A **Format Chart Area** dialog window will appear. The dialog window will vary depending on the part of the chart you selected.
3. *Click* on the **Fill** tab.
4. *Click* the option button that best fits your choice. Addition information may appear depending on your choice of option.
5. *Click* **OK**.

Customizing the Layout of Charts

If you want to customize the layout of your chart, you first select anywhere in the chart or select the chart element that you want to change. Then under **Chart Tools - Layout** tab, you can change labels, axes, and backgrounds.

In the **Labels** group you can add a chart title, add titles to the axis, show legends and add data tables. You can add a chart title on the chart or above the chart.

If you *click* on **Chart Title** the option box lets you select **More Title Options**. Here you can add fill to the title (fill means you can put a color in the Title Box), put a border around the title box, show a shadow, add a glow or make it 3-D.

Under the **Axis Titles** button you can add **Horizontal** or **Vertical Axis Titles**.

Under the **Legend** button you can place the legend at different locations on the chart or remove the legend from the chart.

If you want to put **Data Labels** on the chart, *click* on the **Data Labels** button. Here you have the options for locations to put the data labels or to have no data labels.

Click on the **Data Table** button and you can insert a table with your chart. This is similar to selecting a chart with the table under the **Chart Tools – Design** tab in the **Chart Layouts** group.

In the **Axes** group, *click* a layout option for the Primary Horizontal or Vertical axis or Depth Axis. The Depth axis is only available for certain charts.

Under the **Gridlines** button you can add Primary Horizontal or Vertical gridlines to the chart. For certain charts you can add Depth gridlines.

In the **Background** group, *click* a layout option for the background that you want to change. The options for changing the background depends on the type of chart you are working with. Options for chart walls, floors, and 3-D rotation are available on 3-D charts only.

If you need to add **Trend lines**, **Lines**, **Up/Down Bars**, or **Error Bars** you will find them in the **Analysis** group, *click* a layout option for any lines or bars that you want to add or change. Depending on the chart type, some or all analysis options may not be available.

If you do not see **Chart Tools** or the **Layout** tab, make sure that you have selected a chart.

On the **Layout** tab, you can also find options to add pictures, shapes, or text boxes under the **Insert** group. To change the format of a specific chart element, you can *right-click* that chart element, and then *click* **Format - <Chart element>.** And the Format window will appear.

Customize the formatting of a chart

If you need to change a part of the charts color, text color, align charts, put outlines around part of the chart, you will find those options under the **Chart Tools – Format** tab. To put a border around the chart do the following:

1. Select the chart.
2. Under the **Chart Tools – Format** tab *click* on the **More** drop down arrow next to the **Shape Styles** group examples.
3. A window shows that has both borders and solid colors for the chart.
4. To change borders and background colors do one or more of the following: (Note: You may need to *double-click* on the individual section that you would like to change).

a. To add a border *click* on a border in the **Shape Styles** example box or select **Shape Outline** button next to the examples.
b. To change the color *click* on one of the solid colors or *click* on **Shape Fill** next to the examples.
c. To add a solid color, a picture, gradient or textured color *click* on **Shape Fill** next to the examples and select the option you desire.
d. To add a gradient background, *click* on **Shape Fill** and then *click* on **Gradient**. Then select the shade of gradient. If you want several colors, *click* on the **More Gradient** option at the bottom of the **Gradient** option box. Under **Fill** *click* on **Gradient Fill**. You can change color by changing the Preset color and the Direction options. You can also slide the stops on the **Gradient Stop** slide bar. *Click* **Close** when done.

5. You can also change a section of the chart by *clicking* on the section of the chart or selecting the section under drop down list under the **Chart Tools – Format** tab in the **Current Selection** group. At the top of the **Current Selection** group is a drop down list. The drop down list names the parts of the chart that can be altered. Select the part of the chart you would like to change.

6. Then under **Chart Tools - Format** tab, in the **Current Selection** group, *click* **Format Selection**.
7. If you do not see **Chart Tools** - **Format** tab, make sure that you have selected a chart.
8. The Format window appears. Make your changes here.

☑Tip: Using Pictures instead of color on bar charts.

You can use pictures in a bar on a bar chart instead of using color.

1. Make a bar chart.
2. *Click* on the bar that you want to change. Note that if you only want one of the bars to change you will have to *click twice* on the bar to assure that all the bars in the series are not selected.
3. *Right-Click* on the bar. *Click* on **Format Data Series**.
4. *Click* on **Fill**.
5. Select the **Picture of texture fill**.
6. From the **Insert from**: select **File**.
7. Select the picture you would like. *Click* **OK**.
8. Under **File** button you will find three options:
    a. Stretch
    b. Stack
    c. Stack and Scale with:
9. Make your selection and *click* **Close**.
10. Now your bar is filled with a picture.

Note: You can fill other charts with pictures, but they may not present the data is an easy understandable display.

Save as a Chart Template

If you want to create another chart such as the one that you previously created, you can save the chart as a template that you can use as the basis for other similar charts.

1. Select the chart that you want to save as a template
2. Under **Chart Tools - Design** tab, in the **Type** group, *click* **Save As Template**.
3. If you do not see **Chart Tools**, make sure that you have selected a chart.
4. In the **File name** box, type the name that you want to use for the template.

Unless you specify a different folder, the template file (.crtx) will be saved in the **Charts** folder, and the template becomes available under **Templates** in both the **Insert Chart** dialog box (on the **Insert** tab, in the **Charts** group, the **Dialog Box Launcher**) and the **Change Chart Type** dialog box (on the **Design** tab, in the **Type** group, **Change Chart Type**).

A chart template contains the chart format and stores the colors that are being used when you save the chart as a template. When you use a chart template to create a chart in another workbook, the new chart uses the colors of the chart template — not the colors of the document theme that is currently applied to the workbook. To use the document theme colors instead of the chart template colors, *right-click* the chart area, and then *click* **Reset to Match Style**.

Changing the Data in Charts

As you have seen, if your PowerPoint 2010 presentation contains a chart, you can edit the chart data directly in PowerPoint, whether the chart is embedded in or linked to your presentation. You can also update or refresh the data in a linked chart without having to go to the program in which you created the chart. On the page, select the chart that you want to change. A special ribbon tab is added to the ribbon. The **Chart Tools** tab appears at the top of the PowerPoint window. If you do not see the **Chart Tools** tab or the **Design** tab under it, make sure that you *click* the chart to select it. The **Design** tab under **Chart Tools** is not the same as the default **Design** tab in PowerPoint. The **Chart Tools** tab appears only when a chart is selected, and the **Design, Layout** and **Format** tabs under it provide different commands that relate only to the selected chart. To change the data do the following:

1. Under **Chart Tools - Design** tab, in the **Data** group, *click* **Edit Data.** Microsoft PowerPoint - Excel opens in a new window and displays the worksheet for the selected chart.
2. In the Excel worksheet, *click* the cell that contains the title or the data that you want to change, and then enter the new information.
3. Close the Excel file. PowerPoint refreshes and saves the chart automatically.

Remember that this is not a true Excel worksheet, but rather a special PowerPoint – Excel worksheet.

Insert a Linked Excel Chart

You can insert and link a chart from an Excel workbook into your PowerPoint presentation. When you edit the data in the spreadsheet, the chart on the PowerPoint slide can be easily updated. To insert a linked Excel chart in PowerPoint 2010, do the following:

1. Open the Excel workbook that has the chart that you want.

- The workbook must be saved before the chart data can be linked in the PowerPoint file.
- If you move the Excel file to another folder, the link between the chart in the PowerPoint presentation and the data in the Excel spreadsheet breaks.

2. While still in Excel select the chart. On the **Home** tab, in the **Clipboard** group, *click* **Copy**.
3. Open the PowerPoint presentation that you want and select the slide that you want to insert the chart into.
4. On the **Home** tab in PowerPoint, in the **Clipboard** group, *click* the arrow below **Paste**, and then do one of the following:

- If you want the chart to keep its look and appearance from the Excel file, select **Keep Source Formatting & Link Data**.
- If you want the chart to use the look and appearance of the PowerPoint presentation, select **Use Destination Theme & Link Data**.

When you want to update the data in the PowerPoint file, select the chart, and then under **Chart Tools - Design** tab, in the **Data** group, *click* **Refresh Data**. This can be very tricky to get to work just right.

Insert a Linked Spreadsheet

The linked object in your presentation displays all data from the active, top spreadsheet in the linked Excel workbook. To insert and link a saved Excel spreadsheet onto your PowerPoint slide, do the following:

1. In PowerPoint 2010, on the **Insert** tab, in the **Text** group, *click* **Object**.

2. In the **Insert Object** dialog box, select **Create from file**.
3. *Click* **Browse**, and in the **Browse** dialog box, browse to and then select the Excel workbook that contains the information that you want to insert, and then click **OK**.
4. In the **Insert Object** dialog box, check the selection **Link** box and then *click* **OK**.

To edit a linked Excel spreadsheet, do one of the following:

- To edit the data from within Excel, *right-click* the object on the slide, point to **Linked Worksheet Object**, and select **Edit**.
- To update the data on the slide to match the data in the original Excel file, *right-click* the object on the slide, and *click* **Update Link**.

Insert a linked selection from a spreadsheet

To insert and link a selection of data from a saved Excel spreadsheet, do the following:

1. In Excel, open the workbook containing that data that you want to insert.
2. Select and copy the data that you want. The keyboard shortcut for copy is *CTRL + C*.
3. In PowerPoint, *click* the slide where you want to paste the copied worksheet data.
4. On the **Home** tab, in the **Clipboard** group, *click* the arrow below **Paste**, and select **Paste Special**.

5. In the **Paste Special** dialog box, select the **Paste link** box.
6. Under **As**, select a **Microsoft Excel Worksheet Object**.
7. *Click* **OK**.

Linking an Excel worksheet to a clickable object

Sometimes you would like to open an Excel worksheet while you are giving a presentation. The best way to do this without exiting out of the presentation is to link an object in the presentation to the Excel worksheet.

1. Insert an object, picture, shape or text on the PowerPoint page that you will be talking about the Excel worksheet.
2. While the object is selected, *click* on the **Insert** tab.
3. *Click* on **Hyperlink** under the **Link** group.
4. An **Insert Hyperlink** dialog window will open. Select the Excel worksheet file that you would like to open.
5. *Click* **OK**.

While giving the presentation, move the mouse over the object that is linked to the worksheet. The mouse arrow will change to a hand with a pointing finger. The file name should also be showing. *Click* on the object and the Excel worksheet will open. When you are done with the Excel worksheet; you can either minimize the worksheet or close the worksheet. The PowerPoint presentation will open to the page with the link.

Caution: Keep the Excel file and the PowerPoint file in the same folder. If the two files are separated the link will not open the Excel file. If moving the mouse over the linked object does not change to a hand with a pointing finger or you cannot open the file do the following.

1. While on the page with the linked object (and in a **Slide Show** presentation), hit the **Tab** key. This will highlight the first link on the page.
2. Hit **Enter**.

If this does not work, the keyboard may be programmed differently than the default hot keys. I have seen where Shift F5 opens the linked file. If the computer being used is not yours, you have no way of knowing how the hot keys are programmed. If you cannot open the linked file through the PowerPoint slide show you might have to open it through the file explorer. This is one of the main reasons that you want to practice the presentation prior to giving it in front of an audience.

Copy a Selection of Cells from Excel onto a Slide

Data copied and pasted onto a PowerPoint slide does not automatically update when the data is changed in the Excel workbook, like a chart's data does when the chart is developed in PowerPoint. To paste a copy of a selection of the Excel data onto your PowerPoint slide, do the following:

1. In Excel, open the Excel workbook that contains the information that you want to copy.
2. Select and **copy** the data that you want. The keyboard shortcut for copy is *CTRL + C.*
3. In PowerPoint 2010, *click* the slide where you want to paste the copied worksheet data.
4. On the **Home** tab, in the **Clipboard** group, *click* the arrow below **Paste**.
5. Under **Paste Options**, do one of the following:

- Select **Keep Source Formatting** if you want to copy the data as a PowerPoint table, but want it keep the appearance of the original Excel spreadsheet.

- Select **Use Destination Style**s if you want to copy the data as a PowerPoint table, but want it to assume the appearance of the PowerPoint presentation.
- Select **Embed** if you want to copy the data as information that can be edited in Excel.
- Select **Picture** if you want to copy the data as an un-editable picture.
- Select **Keep Text Only** if you want to copy all the data as a single text box.

Animating a Chart

Not all animation effects can be used with charts, some animation effects that will not work with charts are **Drop, Flip** or **Whip**. Effects that are unavailable for charts will appear dimmed.

How to Animate Charts

1. *Click* on the chart.
2. *Click* the **Animations** tab, in the **Animation** group.
3. For Additional animation effects *click* the drop down arrow on the right side of the animation examples.
4. The whole chart will be animated and move together.

Animation Effect Options

To set the animation effect options, do the following:

1. Select the animated chart that you want to modify.
2. *Click* the **Animations** tab.
3. In the **Advanced Animations** group c*lick* the **Effect Options** button that is to the right of the animation examples. The top part of the drop down list is effects options for the particular animation you are using. The bottom part of the drop down list is **Sequences** for the chart. They are:

- **As One Object** - The animation is applied as if the whole Chart as one picture or object. The chart and its sub-parts all moves together, as if they are one object.
- **By Series** – The bars or lines in the chart will animate by series. All the bars or lines by series animate at the same time. The background, table and titles will first animate then the bars, lines or other chart items will animate.
- **By Category** – The bars or lines in the chart will animate by category. All the bars or lines by category animate at the same time. The background, table and titles will first animate then the bars, lines or other chart items will animate.
- **By Element in Series** - The bars or lines in the chart will animate by series. All the bars or lines by series animate one at a time. The background, table and titles will first animate then the bars,

lines or other chart items will animate. Since the bars and lines animate one at a time, animating this way is slower than animating By Series.

- **By Element in Category** - The bars or lines in the chart will animate by category. All the bars or lines by series animate one at a time. The background, table and titles will first animate then the bars, lines or other chart items will animate. Since the bars and lines animate one at a time, animating this way is slower than animating By Category.

Another way to animate a chart is to select the section from the Animation Pane. To animate using the **Animation Pane** do the following:

1. *Click* on the animated chart.
2. In the **Animation** tab, *click* **Animation Pane** under the **Advanced Animation** group.
3. In the **Animation Pane** list, *click* the drop down arrow to the right of the animation that you want to modify.
4. Select **Effect Options**.
5. In the dialog box, on the **Chart Animation** tab, in the **Group Chart** list, select one of the following options:

- **As One Object** - The animation is applied as if the whole Chart as one picture or object. The chart and its sub-parts all moves together, as if they are one object.
- **By Series** – The bars or lines in the chart will animate by series. All the bars or lines by series

animate at the same time. The background, table and titles will first animate then the bars, lines or other chart items will animate.

- **By Category** – The bars or lines in the chart will animate by category. All the bars or lines by category animate at the same time. The background, table and titles will first animate then the bars, lines or other chart items will animate.
- **By Element in Series** - The bars or lines in the chart will animate by series. All the bars or lines by series animate one at a time. The background, table and titles will first animate then the bars, lines or other chart items will animate. Since the bars and lines animate one at a time, animating this way is slower than animating By Series.
- **By Element in Category** - The bars or lines in the chart will animate by category. All the bars or lines by series animate one at a time. The background, table and titles will first animate then the bars, lines or other chart items will animate. Since the bars and lines animate one at a time, animating this way is slower than animating By Category.

Animation Painter

One of the new features in Microsoft PowerPoint 2010 is the **Animation Painter**. Using the **Animation Painter**, you can easily and quickly copy an animation or several animations from one chart to another.

To copy animations from one chart to another, do the following:

1. Select the chart with the animations that you want to copy.
2. On the **Animations** tab, in the **Advanced Animation** group, *click* **Animation Painter**.
3. *Click* the chart that you want to copy the animations onto.

Removing Animations in Charts

If there is a shape that you do not want to be animated you can remove the animation from that shape as long as you animated the chart with any of the options other than **As One Object.** As long as the chart animation shows the double drop down arrows in the **Animation Pane** window, you can remove the animation from any of the detailed movements.

1. *Click* the chart that you want to remove an animation.
2. *Click* on the **Animation Pane** tab, under the Advanced Animation group, under the **Animation** tab.
3. In the **Animation Pane**, *click* on the double down arrows to open up the individual animations.
4. *Click* on the Animation you want to remove. This can be very hard to determine, you will have to know the order in which the chart objects are animated, because the names given in the **Animation Pane** do not identify any one particular shape.

5. *Click* on the right drop down arrow.
6. *Click* on **Remove**.

Be careful when removing an animation on a chart. You cannot just add the animation back. To add the animation back to the chart you will have to redo the animation for the complete chart.

You can also remove multiple, specific animation effects. *Press and hold CTRL*, and then in the **Animation Task** pane, select each animation effect that you want to remove, *right-click* one of the selected effects and select **Remove**.

Remove an animation from the Chart

1. *Click* on the chart with the animation that you want to remove.
2. On the **Animations** tab, in the **Animation** group *click* **None**. If you don't see **None**, *click* the drop down arrow on the right side of the animation example for more options. **None** is mostly the top option.

Timing or Effect Options

You can customize the timing of animation effects in Microsoft PowerPoint 2010, including the timing and order with which they start, and whether they repeat.

To set the start time for an animation effect, follow these steps:

1. *Click* on the chart that you want to set the timing.
2. On the **Animations** tab, in the **Timing** group, do one of the following:

- To start the animation effect when you *click* the slide, select **Start:** On Click
- To start the animation effect at the same time as the previous effect in the list (that is, one *click* executes multiple animation effects), select **Start:** With Previous
- To start the animation effect immediately after the previous effect in the list finishes playing (that is, you do not have to *click* again to make the next animation effect start), select **Start:** After Previous

Duration of /or Delaying Animation Effects

1. *Click* on the chart that contains the animation effect for which you want to set a delay or other timing option.
2. On the **Animations** tab, in the **Timing** group, do one or more of the following:

- To specify the length of an animation effect, enter a number in the **Duration** box.
- To create a delay between the end of one animation effect and the start of a new animation effect, enter a number in the **Delay** box.

Repeat or rewind an animation effect

You can make an animation repeat a number of times (2, 3, 4, 5, or 10 times), **Until Next Click**, or **Until End of Slide**. To make an animation effect or sequence of effects repeat or return to its original position, follow these steps:

1. *Click* on the chart that you want to repeat.
2. On the **Animations** tab, in the **Animation** group, *click* on the arrow in the lower right-hand corner of the Animation group box. This is called **Show Additional Effect Options** launcher.
3. A new window appears, *click* the **Timing** tab, and then do one or more of the following:

- To select a repeat option *click* on the **Repeat** drop down arrow, and select an option in the **Repeat** list.
- To automatically return an animation effect to its original look and location after it plays, select the **Rewind when done playing** check box. In some cases this will make the SmartArt disappear after the animation.

Changing the Animation Order

Animated charts on a slide display a number indicating the order in which the object's animation plays. Charts are different than other animated objects when it comes to changing the order of the animation. Depending on the type of chart, different options are available for the animation. To see the options available for animation on a chart follow these steps:

1. C*lick* on the animated chart.
2. *Click* on the **Animations** tab.
3. On the **Animations** tab, in the **Animation** group, *click* on the arrow in the lower right-hand corner of

the Animation group box. This is called **Show Additional Effect Options** launcher.

4. A dialog window will open. The name of the dialog window will vary, depending on the chart and the animation. *Click* on the **Chart Animation** tab.
5. In the **Group Chart** drop down box will be the options that you can select.

Not all options are available for all charts. Here are some of the selections that you will have:

- **As One Object -** The animation is applied as if the whole Chart as one picture or object. The chart and its sub-parts all moves together, as if they are one object.
- **By Series** – The bars or lines in the chart will animate by series. All the bars or lines by series animate at the same time. The background, table and titles will first animate then the bars, lines or other chart items will animate.
- **By Category** – The bars or lines in the chart will animate by category. All the bars or lines by category animate at the same time. The background, table and titles will first animate then the bars, lines or other chart items will animate.
- **By Element in Series** - The bars or lines in the chart will animate by series. All the bars or lines by series animate one at a time. The background, table and titles will first animate then the bars, lines or other chart items will animate. Since the

bars and lines animate one at a time, animating this way is slower than animating By Series.

- **By Element in Category** - The bars or lines in the chart will animate by category. All the bars or lines by series animate one at a time. The background, table and titles will first animate then the bars, lines or other chart items will animate. Since the bars and lines animate one at a time, animating this way is slower than animating By Category.

Trigger an Animation Effect

With triggers, you can make an animation effect occur during a slide show when you *click* an object on the slide or when you play a specific part of a video. To set a trigger on a *click*, follow these steps:

1. Select the object that has the animation that you want to trigger.
2. On the **Animations** tab, in the **Advanced Animation** group, *click* **Trigger**.
3. *Click* **On Click of**, and select the object that you want to trigger the animation. Because of their placeholders some charts are limited.

Disable Animations from Playing

If you want to disable the animation from playing but not delete the animation follow these steps:

1. *Click* on the **Slide Show** tab.
2. Under the **Set Up** group, *click* **Set Up Slide Show**.

3. In the **Set Up Show** dialog box, under **Show options**, select the **Show without animation** check box.
4. *Click* **OK**.

Chapter 9 Text & WordArt

I am going to put text and WordArt in the same section. There is a little difference between the two, but basically you can do the same things to both. Some of the design work is easier in WordArt and they may look more professional, but overall the basics are about the same.

There are several ways to add text to PowerPoint slides.

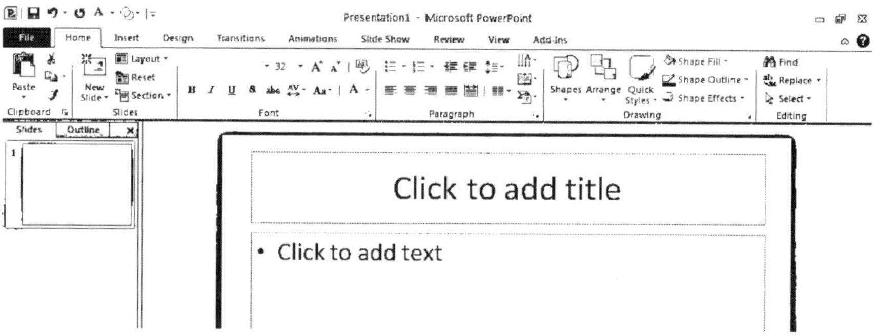

The first way is, if a text box already exists, is to *double click* within the text box and start typing.

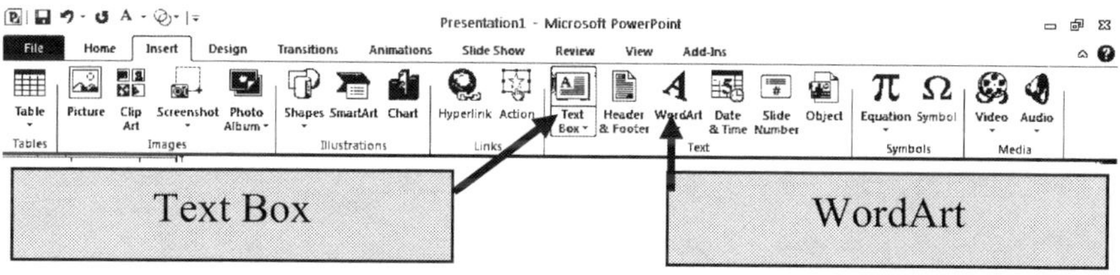

If no text box already exists on the slide do the following:

1. *Click* on the **Insert** tab.
2. *Click* on **Text Box (WordArt).**
3. There are two options: **Horizontal Text Box** and **Vertical Text Box**. *Click* on the type of text box

you would like. In WordArt a gallery dialog window opens up.

4. On the slide, *click and drag* at the location that you want the text box. In WordArt the text box is placed in the middle of the slide.
5. A cursor will be flashing in an empty text box. Start typing. If you are using WordArt, *click* inside the box to change the text.

Change Fonts

To change the text's fonts, color or location within the text box, do the following:

This process is similar to Word.

1. Highlight the word (text), and *click* on the **Home** tab.
2. Under the **Paragraph** group, you can:

- Bullet or number the texts list.
- Decrease or Increase the list level.
- Increase or decrease line spacing.
- Align text left, center, right, justified or distribute the text.
- Split the text into columns.
- Change the orientation of the text. Under **Text Direction** you can *click* on **More Options** and the **Format Text Effects** window will open. Make sure that the **Text Box** tab is selected

- Align text to the top, middle, or bottom of the shape.
- Convert the test to SmartArt.

Under the Font group, where you can:

- Change the type of fonts.
- Change the size of the fonts.
- Bold, italic, or underline the text.
- Shadow the text.
- Strikethrough the text.
- Space out the characters.
- Change case of the text.
- Increase or decrease the fonts by clicking on the large A or small A.
- Change the text color.
- Or Clear all formatting.

☑Tip: Use of Text

Many professional presenters have rules for using text and bullet points. They believe that you should use very little text and use pictures instead. Also they believe you should never use bullet points. I think there are times when you have to use text and times when bullet points are the best way to present the text. But instead of over using the bullet dot, you should be more creative and use pictures or symbols. It is easy to change the ever-boring bullet dots to something neat and entertaining.

1. *Click* on the bullet text.
2. Under the **Home** tab, *click* on the **Bullets** drop down arrow, under the **Paragraph** group.

3. *Click* on **Bullets and Numbering**.
4. **Click** on either **Pictures** or **Customize**.
5. Under **Pictures**:
    a. A **Picture Bullet** dialog window will open.
    b. Either select one of the pictures provided or *click* on **Import**.
    c. If you selected **Import**, the **Add Clip to Organizer** dialog window will open.
    d. Select a picture from the window and *click* **Add**.
    e. Once the picture in added to the **Picture Bullet** dialog window, *click* **OK**.
6. Under **Customize**:
    a. The **Symbol** dialog window will open.
    b. *Click* on the symbol you want.
    c. *Click* **OK**.
7. Now your bullets are special.

☑Tip: Change Bullet point text to SmartArt.

You can also make bullet point text more interesting by changing them to SmartArt.

1. *Right-click* on the bulleted text.
2. *Click* on **Convert to SmartArt**.
3. *Click* on the SmartArt design you like.
4. Now your bulleted text has style.

Change Text Box Background

To change the background of the text box do the following:

1. *Click* on the text box.
2. *Click* on **Drawing Tools – Format**.
3. Under the **Shape Styles** group, *click* on **Shape Fill**.
4. Select the color you would like.
5. The text box's background changes to the color you selected.

Adding Border to Text Box

To add a border to the text box follow these steps:

1. *Click* on the Text Box.
2. *Click* on **Drawing Tools – Format** tab.
3. Under the **Shape Styles** group, *click* on **Shape Outline.**
4. *Click* on the color that you want the border to be.
5. *Click* on **Shape Outline** again.
6. Go down to **Weight**. A drop down list box opens.
7. *Click* on the weight that you want the text box to have.
8. The text box now has a colored border with the border weight you have chosen.

Change Text Color

To change the text color, do the following:

1. Highlight the text in the text box.
2. *Click* on **Drawing Tools – Format**.
3. Under the **WordArt Styles** group, *click* on **Text Fill**.
4. *Click* the color that you want the text to be.
5. The text will change to the color you selected.

☑**Tip: Change Text Box Shape**

You can change the shape of a text box. Do the following to change the shape of a text box:

1. *Click* on the text box.
2. Under **Drawing Tools – Format**, *click* **Edit Shape** in the **Insert Shapes** group.
3. *Click* **Change Shape**.
4. *Click* on a shape. The Rectangle shapes work great.
5. *Click* **Edit Points** again. The corners of the text box will change to black boxes. If **Edit Points** is dimmed, you may have to change shapes. Also **Edit Points** may be dimmed if you have more than one text box selected.
6. *Click* on one of the black boxes. The black box that you *clicked* has added two white boxes along the border of the text box.

7. *Click and drag* one of the white boxes. When you click on the white box it changes to a box with four arrows. When you move a white box the text box border on either side of the black dot change shape.
8. You can also *click and drag* one of the black boxes. All the corner boxes will stay stable while you move the one corner.

☑**Tip: Putting pictures in Text.**

You can put a picture in the text, as long as the text is big enough to identify the picture. Otherwise the picture will look only as a color or texture.

1. Type your text and make the text big and bold.
2. Highlight the text.
3. *Click* on **Drawing Tools – Format** tab.
4. *Click* on the drop down arrow next to **Text Fill** under the **WordArt Styles** group.
5. *Click* **Picture**.
6. Select your picture and *click* on **Insert**.
7. Now the text is filled with a picture. If you do not see your picture you may have to enlarge the text fonts.
8. To change the location of the picture in the text go back into the **Format Text Effects** dialog window.
    a. Highlight the text and *right-click* on the text.
    b. *Click* on **Format Text Effects**.
    c. *Click* **Text Fill**.

9. Under the **Insert From – File** button, check the box for **Tile Picture as Texture**. A **Tiling Options** area opens.
10. Next to **Alignment** *click* on the drop down arrow and select different alignments to move the picture.
11. You can also change the **Picture Transparent** in the **Format Text Effects** dialog window.

Add Alternative Text

For shapes, pictures, charts, tables, SmartArt graphics, or other objects you can have alternative text, which makes it easy to change text to placeholders. For example, if you have a certificate that you would like to design and want to only change the names of the students that are being awarded the certificate, you would use the alternative text to make the job of printing the certificates easy. To make alternative text follow these steps:

1. *Right-click* the text box that you would like to add alternative text to.
2. At the bottom of the drop down box is a **Format Shape** command. *Click* on **Format Shape.**
3. A **Format Shape** window appears. Go to the bottom of the options and *click* on **Alt Text**.
4. If you want, in the **Title** box, enter a brief summary. This box should only be filled in if you are entering a detailed or long explanation in the **Description** box.
5. In the **Description** box, enter an explanation of the shape, picture, chart, table, SmartArt graphic, or other object. This box should always be filled in.

Unless you have a complex chart or table, you will usually want to enter text in just the **Description** box. When you have complex content to describe, then filling in the **Title** field is useful so reading the full description is not necessary unless desired.

Add a Text Placeholder

If you create templates for others to use to create new presentations, you can overwrite the text in the default placeholders by adding custom prompt text.
There is a difference between how you use a text placeholder versus a text box in the **Slide Master** view. When you want users of your template to enter specific types of information into placeholders, add a text placeholder from within **Slide Master** view. The custom prompt text in a text placeholder disappears when the user begins typing. If you want your template to contain permanent and un-editable text, add a text box in **Slide Master** view. If you add a text box in **Normal** view, the text is editable by anyone.

The custom prompt text provides instructions about what type of information to enter.

Align Text Boxes

Many times it is hard to get pictures, shapes or text boxes to line up in a straight row or column. PowerPoint makes it easy to align objects.

1. *Click* on the first object, whether a picture, shape, text box or chart.
2. Use either the *Shift – Click* method or the *Ctrl – Click* method to select all the objects that you want to align.
3. *Click* on the **Drawing Tools – Format** tab.

4. Under the **Arrange** group, *click* on **Align**.
5. When **Align** list appears then select the alignment that you would like.

Text box or WordArt as a Watermark

You can use text or WordArt as a watermark. Using text or WordArt as a watermark is better than a picture or design, because you can make the text transparent and it can be on top of the other items on the slide. To make text or WordArt watermarks do the following:

1. Highlight the text of WordArt that you would like to make a watermark.
2. Under the **Drawing Tools – Format**, *click* on **Text Fill** in the **WordArt Styles** group.
3. *Click* on **Texture**
4. *Click* on **More Textures** (at the bottom of the pop-up texture window).
5. The **Format Text Effects** dialog window opens. *Click* on the **Text Fill** tab (on the left side of the window).
6. *Click* on **Solid Fill**.
7. Move the slider next to **Transparency** to around 75 or greater.
8. *Click* **Close**.

If you are making a WordArt or text with a gradient fill, you can also:

1. Change the **Brightness**

2. And adjust the **Gradient Stops**. Play with the **Brightness, Transparency**, and the **Gradient Stops** to get the right appearance.

By doing a watermark this way you do not have to move the text or WordArt to the back of the slide.

Animating Text

With animation you can have more control of a presentation and how you want it delivered. Using animation is a great way to focus on important points, to control the flow of information, and to increase viewer interest in your presentation. You can apply animation effects to text, pictures, charts, shapes or objects on individual slides. Animation can also be added to the slide master, or to placeholders on custom slide layouts. The most common types of animation effects include entrances and exits. There are four different kinds of animation effects in PowerPoint 2010:

Entrance effects. These are marked in green and used to bring your item into the screen. You can make an object fade gradually into focus, fly onto the slide from an edge, or bounce into view. By using the Effect Options you can change the direction, or change the sequence of the animation.

Exit effects. These effects are marked in red and used to remove an item from the screen. They can include making an object fly off of the slide, disappear from view, or spiral off of the slide. Once again by using the Effect Option you can change the direction or sequence.

Emphasis effects. These are marked in yellow and are used to highlight an item. Examples of these effects include making an object shrink or grow in size, change color, or spin on its center.

Motion Paths. These are marked with a dotted line. You can use these effects to make an object move up or down, left or right, or in a star or circular pattern (among other effects). Motion paths can be altered using the **Effect Options** and **Edit Points**.

You can use any animation by itself or combine multiple effects together. For instance, you can make a line of text fly in from the left while it grows in size by applying a Fly In entrance effect and a Grow/Shrink emphasis effect to it. If you want to add an animation to a text box that already has an animation make sure that you first select **Add Animation** button in the **Advanced Animation** group under the **Picture Tools – Format** tab. If you just select a new animation, the old animation will be replaced.

Viewing Animations Pane

You can view the list of all the animations on the slide in the **Animation Task Pane**. The **Animation Task Pane** shows important information about an animation effect, such as: the type of effect, the order of multiple effects in relation to one another, the name of the object affected, and the duration of the effect.

To open the **Animation Task Pane**, *click* on the **Animations** tab, in the **Advanced Animation** group, *click* **Animation Pane.**

1. In the task pane, numbers indicate the order in which the animation effects play. The numbers in the task pane correspond to the numbered tags that are displayed on the slide.
2. Timelines represent the duration of the effects.
3. Icons represent the type of animation effect. They are color coded for **Entrance, Exit,** and **Emphasis**.
4. Select an item in the list to see the menu icon (down arrow), and then *click* the icon to reveal the menu.

5. Effects appear in the **Animation Task Pane** in the order that you add them. To move an item up or down in sequence use the **Re-Order** buttons at the bottom of the **Animation Pane**.
6. You can also view the icons that indicate the start of the animation effects in relation to the other events on the slide; this is called the **Advanced Timeline**. To view the start timing icons for all animations, *click* the menu icon next to an animation effect and select **Hide Advanced Timeline**.

There are several ways to start the animation and there are several types of icons that indicate the start timing of animation effects. Choices include the following:

- **Start On Click:** (🖱 - mouse icon): The animation begins when you *click* the mouse.
- **Start With Previous:** (✓ - check mark): The animation effect starts playing at the same time as the previous effect in the list. This setting combines multiple effects at the same time.
- **Start After Previous:** (🕓 - clock icon): The animation effect begins immediately after the previous effect in the list finishes playing.

Effect Options, Timing, or Order for an Animation

The **Effects Options** vary depending on the animation used. To set the **Effect Options** for an animation follow these steps:

1. *Click* on the **Animations** tab.
2. In the **Animation** group, *click* the arrow to the right of **Effect Options.**
3. *Click* the option that you want.

On the **Animation** tab under the **Timing** group you can specify the start, duration, or delay timing for an animation.

- To set the **Start Timing** for an animation, in the **Timing** group, *click* the arrow to the right of the **Start** menu and select the timing that you want.
- To set the **Duration** of how long the animation will run, in the **Timing** group, enter the number of seconds that you want in the **Duration** box.
- To set a **Delay** before the animation begins, in the **Timing** group, enter the number of seconds that you want in the **Delay** box.

Changing the Order of Animations

You can change the order in which the animation takes pales.

1. To **re-order** an animation in the list, in the **Animation Pane**, select the animation that you want to re-order.
2. *Click* the **Animations** tab, in the **Timing** group, under **Reorder Animation**, either:

- Select **Move Earlier** to make the animation occur before another animation in the list.
- Select **Move Later** to make the animation occur after another animation in the list.

- You can also *click and drag* the animation up or down in the **Animation Pane**.
- Or *click* on the animation that you want to re-order and go to the bottom of the **Animation Pane** and **click** the up or down arrow buttons on either side of the **Re-Order** command.

Test your animation effect

After you add one or more animation effects, to validate that they work, on the **Animations** tab, in the **Preview** group, *click* **Preview**.

For simple animation follow these steps:

1. *Click* on the text, picture or shape that you want to animate.
2. *Click* on the **Animation** tab
3. Under the **Animation** group you will see some entrance animations.
4. *Click* the drop down arrow on the right side of the group to see more animations.
5. *Click* on the animation that you would like
6. PowerPoint will demonstrate the animation. And put a number next to the text, picture or shape.
7. Once you add the animation to the text you can click on **Preview** under the **Animation** tab.

Open the Animation Pane

If you would like to see all the animated motion entrances, exits and motion paths that are on the present page, you will need to open the **Animation Pane**.

1. *Click* on the **Animation** tab.
2. Under the **Advanced Animation** group, *click* on **Animation Pane**. The **Animation Pane** will open on the right side of the screen. The animation events are number showing the order of the events. When you *click* on one of the animated event a drop down menu appears. Here is where you can change how you want the event to be activated, either by a click, with a previous, after the previous or with timing. At the top of the **Animation Pane** is a Play button for you to review the animation.

Animate along a Motion Path

In PowerPoint you are not limited to the preset motions paths that are determined by the animation effect you choose. You can tell the object where you want it to go.

1. *Click* the object or text to which you want to add a motion path. The path that you apply is followed by the center of the object or text bullet.
2. On the **Animations** tab, in the **Animations** group, *click* on the drop down arrow on the right side of the group.
3. Toward the bottom of the drop down window you will find a section labeled **Motion Paths**.
4. *Click* on the **Motion Path** that you would like.
5. PowerPoint will demonstrate the motion path, put a number by the item that you animated and show the path that the item will follow.

6. You can further adjust the motion path by *clicking* on **Effect Options.**
7. At the bottom of the **Effect Options** drop down menu is an **Edit Points** command.
8. *Click* on the **Edit Points,** and black dots are located on the motion path.
9. *Click* on one of the black dots and *drag* to a new location, changing the motion path.
10. There are also two new white boxes, *clicking* on one of the white boxes and *dragging* to a new location will move the motion path, giving you more flexibility to adjust the motion path to any shape you would like.
11. To reverse the path, *right-click* on the green arrow on the motion path and select **Reverse Path Direction**.
12. To see the complete animation and sound for the slide, on the **Animations** tab, in the **Preview** group, *click* **Preview.**

You can move the motion path. *Click* on the motion path, when the pointer shows a four-way arrow, *click and drag* the motion path where you want it.

The **Shapes and Loops** paths are closed, meaning the object returns to its starting point. To return to the starting point with an open path, such as Lines, Arcs, Turns or Custom Path, *right-click* the path and then *click* **Close Path**. A linear path is added from the previous end point to the starting point.

Any part of the path, including the beginning or ending point, can operate off the slide.

To activate the trigger command, reselect the text in the text box. On the **Animations** tab, in the **Advanced Animation** group, in the **Trigger** list, select **On Bookmark**, and then *click* the bookmark that corresponds to the time you want the text box to fade in.

Apply multiple animation effects to a single object

To apply multiple animations onto the same object, do the following:

1. Select the text or object that you want to add multiple animations.
2. On the **Animations** tab, in the **Advanced Animation** group, *click* **Add Animation**.

If you try to add an animation by *clicking* on the text and then *clicking* on a different animation you will replace the first animation.

Chapter 10 Header & Footer

You can add headers and footers to your presentation (such as your presentation's title, the presenter's name, a file name, company name, and more) to one or more slides, handouts, or notes pages in your presentation.

Add Footer to a slide

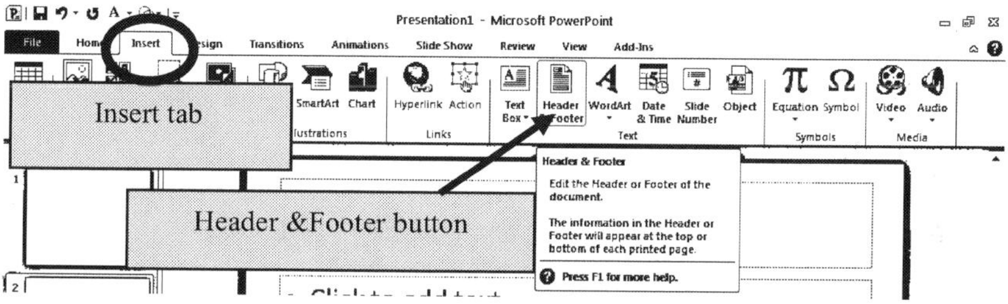

1. On the **Insert** tab, in the **Text** group, *click* **Header & Footer**.
2. In the **Header and Footer** dialog box, on the **Slide** tab, select the **Footer** check box, and then type the text that you want to appear in the center bottom of the slide.
3. To keep the text in the footer from appearing on the title slide, select the **Don't show on title slide** check box.
4. Do one of the following:

- To display footer information on the selected slide only, *click* **Apply**.
- To display footer information on all of the slides in your presentation, *click* **Apply to All**.

Add a Header or Footer to a Handout or Notes Page

1. On the **Insert** tab, in the **Text** group, *click* **Header & Footer**.
2. In the **Header and Footer** dialog box, on the **Notes and Handouts** tab, select the **Header** or **Footer** check box, or both, and then type the text that you want to appear in the center top (header) or center bottom (footer) of each notes page or handout.
3. *Click* **Apply to all**.

The **Preview** box, located in the **Header and Footer** dialog box, displays the header and footer information in the location that the slide, handout, or notes page will display it.

Adding Date and Time

You can *click* on **Date & Time** under the **Insert** tab, in the **Text** group, and the **Header and Footer** dialog window will open. Or you can *click* **Header & Footer** and follow these steps.

1. On the **Insert** tab, in the **Text** group, *click* **Header & Footer**.
2. In the **Header and Footer** dialog box, on the **Slide** tab, select the **Date and Time** check box and then select **Update Automatically** or **Fixed.** Use the drop down box to select the format that you would like to show. Select the Language.
3. *Click* **Apply to all** to add all the slides or *click* **Apply** to only apply to the selected slide.

The **Preview** box, located in the **Header and Footer** dialog box, displays the header and footer information in the location that the slide, handout, or notes page will display it.

Adding Slide Number

You can add slide numbers, notes page numbers, and the date and time to your presentation by using the ribbon commands.

1. On the **Insert** tab, in the **Text** group, click on **Date & Time,** or **Slide Number**.
2. The **Header and Footer** dialog window will appear. *Click* on the check box that you would like to add. For **Date and Tim**e select either **Update Automatically** or **Fixed**.
3. If you want to add slide numbers, *click* the **Slide** tab, and then select the **Slide Number** check box.
4. If you want to add notes page numbers, *click* the **Notes and Handouts** tab, and then select the **Page Number** check box.
5. If you want to add numbers to all of the slides or notes pages in your presentation, *click* **Apply to All**.

Changing Slide Start Number

If you want to change the starting slide number, do the following:

1. On the **Design** tab, in the **Page Setup** group, *click* **Page Setup**.
2. In the **Number Slides From** box, enter the number that you want to start from.

If you do not want the title page to have a number, but you want all the other slides to be numbered do the following:

1. *Click* on the second slide. (The slide that you would like to start the numbering).
2. *Click* on the **Insert** tab.
3. Under the **Text** group, *click* on the **Slide Number.** Note: if the cursor is in a text box, the page number will be placed inside the text box. If there are not objects highlighted the **Header and Footer** dialog window will open.
4. On the **Slide** tab check the box next to **Slide Number**.
5. *Click* **Apply to All**.
6. Now *click* on the title page (first page), *click* on the **Insert** tab.
7. Under the **Text** group, *click* on the **Slide Number**.
8. Uncheck the box next to **Slide Number**.
9. *Click* **Apply**.

Now the title page should not have a number at the bottom of the slide but all the other slides should be numbered.

How to move Headers and Footers

You can relocate headers and footer, Date & Time, and Slide Numbers. On the slide, *click* on the header or footer that you want to move. It should now have a text box around it. It can now be moved, sized or rotated like any other text box.

Deleting Header and Footer from Slides

1. On the **Insert** tab, in the **Text** group, *click* **Header & Footer.**
2. In the **Header and Footer** dialog box, on the **Slide** tab, clear the check boxes for the options that you want to delete from the header or footer.
3. *Click* **Apply** or **Apply to All**. *Click* **Apply** if you only want to change only the slide that you are presently on, and **Apply to All** if you want to change all the slides.

Deleting Header and Footer from Notes and Handouts

1. *Click* the slide that you want to delete the header or footer information from.
2. On the **Insert** tab, in the **Text** group, *click* **Header & Footer**.
3. In the **Header and Footer** dialog box, on the **Notes and Handouts** tab, clear the check boxes for the options that you want to delete from the header or footer.
4. *Click* **Apply to All**.

Chapter 11 Background

Backgrounds can add a touch of class to a presentation. White and black backgrounds are not that appealing and used with the wrong color of text can be hard on the eyes and hard to read. Backgrounds can be pictures, company logos, solid colors, designs or gradient colors. Great consideration should be given when selecting a background. Make sure that the text is easy to read with the background, make sure the background is easy on the eyes, and make sure the background coordinates with your message.

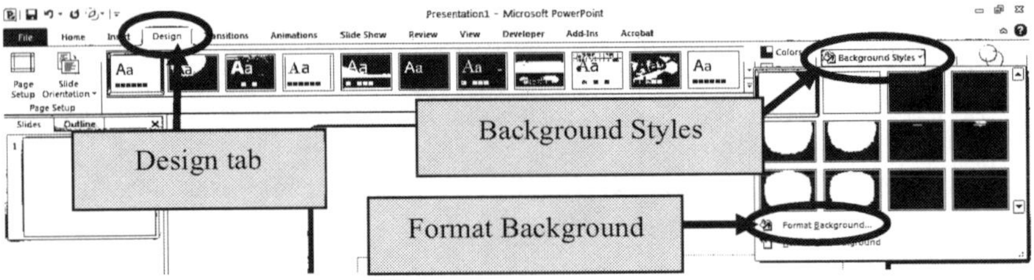

Backgrounds can be a solid color, a texture, and a design from a template or a picture. To make a background a solid color, follow these steps:

1. *Click* on the **Design** tab.
2. *Click* on **Background Styles** under the **Background** group.
3. Select the background color that is shown, mostly this is blue.
4. *Click* on **Colors** under the **Themes** group (still under the **Design** tab). A **Custom theme color** window appears.
5. Move your mouse down the list. The slide background will change.

6. *Click* the one that you want.
7. All the slides change to the color you selected.

Changing Slide's Background

You can change each page's background to different colors or textures.

1. *Click* on the **Design** tab.
2. *Click* on **Background Styles** under the **Background** group.
3. *Click* on **Format Background** (below the color selections). The **Format Background** window appears.
4. On the left side of the window *click* **Fill**.
5. *Click* on **Solid Fill**. You can also *click* on **Gradient Fill.**
6. *Click* on the drop down box next to **Color**. If you *clicked* on **Gradient Fill**, then *clicking* on the drop down box next to **Color** (Under Gradient Stops) will bring up a second color for the gradient mix. The controls on the slider will control how much of each color is used in the gradient mix.
7. Select a color.
8. To change the background transparency, move the **Transparency** slider. You can vary the percentage of transparency from 0% (fully opaque, the default setting) to 100% (fully transparent).

9. *Click* **Close**. If you *click* on **Apply to All** then all the slides will change, then *click* **Close**.

To change to a color that is not in the theme colors, *click* **More Colors**, and then either *click* the color that you want on the **Standard** tab, or mix your own color on the **Custom** tab. Custom colors and colors on the **Standard** tab are not updated if you later change the document theme.

Adding Texture as a Background

You can add a texture as a background. The texture can be added to all the slides or individual slides. Follow these steps:

1. *Click* on **Design** tab
2. *Click* on **Background Styles** under the **Background** group.
3. *Click* on **Format Background** (under the color examples). A **Format Background** window will appear.
4. Under the **Fill** tab, select **Picture or Texture Fill.**
5. *Click* on the drop down arrow next to **Texture**.
6. Select the texture you like. The background on the slide changes.
7. *Click* **Close** if you want to only apply the texture to the single slide. *Click* **Apply to All** if you want to apply the texture to all the slides.

If you do not like any of the textures you can pick one from your files. Instead of *clicking* on the drop down arrow next to **Texture**, you would *click* on **File**, under the **Insert From**. Or you can add a **Clip Art** as the background. *Click* **Clip Art** under the **Insert From**. You can also alter the texture by checking the box next to Tile Picture as Texture or adjusting the **Transparency** slide bar.

Adding a Theme

PowerPoint 2010 comes with many pre-designed themes. You can change the color of the templates and add effects to the templates. If you have already set up your presentation to the layout that you want, then you need to be careful applying a theme. Themes will change the layout of the page, depending on the theme layout.

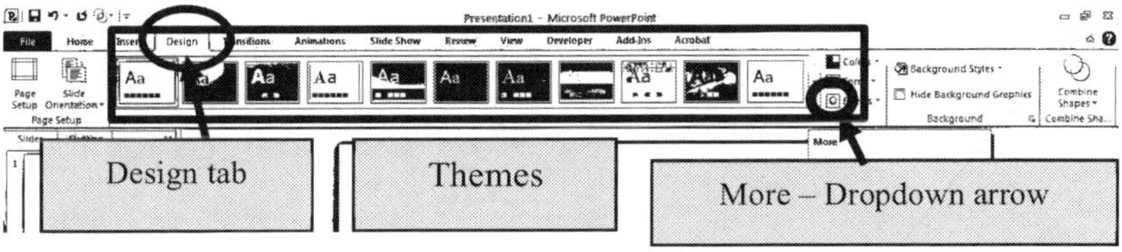

To add a template to the slides do the following:

1. *Click* on **Design** tab. Under the **Themes** group select a template theme. If you do not see one you like, *click* on the drop down arrow to the right of the theme examples.
2. *Click* on the theme you like.
3. The theme is applied to all the slides.

To change the themes color *click* on **Color** on the right side of the **Themes** group. A **Custom color** menu bar appears. As you move your mouse over the menu the slide will change colors. Select the color you like and all the slides will change. Some themes will not change the background color, but will only change the color of the graphics on the slide.

To change the theme effects *click* on **Effects** on the right side of the **Themes** group. Sometimes this will make very little change to the theme; it depends on the SmartArt, shapes or charts used in the presentation. You can download more themes from the Internet and from

Microsoft's web site. To find more themes on the Internet, type in "PowerPoint Themes" in your search engine.

Pictures as Backgrounds

There are several ways to insert a picture as a background. Here are several ways to add pictures as background and then adjust them.

1. *Click* on the **Design** tab.
2. *Click* on **Background Styles** under the **Background** group.
3. *Click* on **Format Background**.
4. *Click* on **Fill** in the left hand menu.
5. *Click* on **Picture or Texture Fill.**
6. Under the **Insert From**: *click* on **File**.
7. Find the picture you want as a background.
8. *Click* **Insert**.
9. *Click* **Close** to apply only to one slide or *click* **Apply to All** to apply to all the slides.

A second way to add a picture as a background is as follows:

1. *Click* on **Insert** tab then **Picture**.
2. Select the picture from your file; even a Clip Art can be selected.
3. *Click* **Insert**
4. Resize the picture to fill the page.
5. *Click* on the special ribbon tab **Picture Tools – Format.**
6. Under the **Arrange** group, *click* on the **Send Backwards** drop down arrow.

7. *Click* on **Send to Back**.
8. To move picture backwards on the screen, *right-click* on the picture, *click* **Order** tab and *click* either **Send to Back** or **Send Backward**. **Sent to Back** will move the picture behind any other text or design (including other pictures).

Alter Pictures

If you want to change a picture that was inserted as a picture and not inserted as a background, you will have to select the picture. To alter the picture when added this way you can go to the **Corrections and Color** tabs under the **Adjust** group. The **Corrections and Color** tabs are under the **Picture Tools – Format** tab.

Alter the Transparency of a Picture

To alter the picture that is used as a background, *click* on the slide that has the picture.

1. *Click* on the **Design** tab.
2. *Click* **Background Styles** under the **Background** group.
3. *Click* **Format Background**.
4. *Click* on **Fill**. Under **Stretch Options** you can adjust the **Transparency** slider bars that will adjust the picture.

Picture Correction

Many times when you use a picture as a background you want to adjust the softness or the contrast of the picture, or you might want to change the color of the picture.

Make sure that the picture is the desired size, most the time this will be the full size of the page.

☑**Tip: Picture as a background or picture enlarged to fill background.**

If you use a picture for a background, there are several choices that you have. There is a difference between using a picture as a background and enlarging a picture to fill the background. A picture as a background will have a **Format Background** dialog window that can be opened and the **Transparency** can be changed under the **Fill** tab. Under **Picture Corrections** the picture can be altered by: changing the **Sharpen and Soften**, changing the **Brightness and Contrast** or make more changes by using the **Picture Color** and **Artistic Effects** tabs.

These tools are also available if you set a picture on a slide and enlarge it to fill the background. These tools would be available under the **Picture Tools – Format** tab. But with this choice you can have options for borders, picture frames and you can rotate the picture.

Another concern with setting a picture as a background is that it may be changed if you use the **Background Styles** choices. When you use the drop down arrow next to the **Background Styles** button under the **Design** tab, you would change the background picture to the background style that you selected in the **Background Style** window.

Changing the Color

In PowerPoint you can alter the picture by changing the color or adding effects to the picture. If you inserted a picture and then resized it and moved it toward the back, you can do the following:

1. *Click* on the picture.
2. *Click* on **Picture Tools – Format** tab.
3. Under the **Adjust** group, *click* **Color**. A **Color Saturation** dialog window opens.

4. You can make changes to:

- **Color Saturation**. The saturation is scaled from 0% to 400%
- **Color Tone**. This is given in Temperature xxxxx K.
- **Recolor**. Changes color tent of the picture.
- **More Variation**. This opens a Theme Color dialog window.
- **Set Transparent Color**. This lets you select one color on the picture and makes it transparent. Only one color can be transparent on a picture.
- **Picture Color Options**. This opens a Format Picture dialog window, with options to change the picture.

Sharpen, Soften, or Change Brightness and Contrast.

You can make pictures sharper or softer by using the **Corrections** tools. Under the **Correction** tool is also the option to brighten pictures.

1. *Click* on the picture.
2. *Click* on **Picture Tools – Format** tab.
3. Under the **Adjust** group, *click* **Corrections**.
4. The **Sharpen and Soften** dialog window opens. Here you can make changes to the pictures contrast by adjusting the tone of the picture.
5. You can make further adjustment to a picture by doing the following:
   a. *Click* on the **Corrections** tab.
   b. C*lick* on **Picture Correction Options** at the bottom of the **Sharpen and Soften** dialog

window. The **Format Picture** dialog window opens where you can adjust the picture further.

The **Artistic Effects** tab can add further effects to the picture. Under the **Artistic Effects** are options for Pencil Grayscale, Line Drawing, Blur, Paint Strokes, Chalk Sketch, Light Screen, Watercolor Sponge, Film Grain, Glass and many more.

If the picture was inserted as a background, adjustments can be made in the Format Background dialog window.

1. *Click* **Design**
2. *Click* **Background Styles** in the **Background** group.
3. The **Form Background** dialog window opens.
4. Under the **Picture Corrections** tab make adjustments to:
    a. Sharpen and Soften
    b. Brightness and Contrast
5. Under **Picture Color** tab make adjustments to:
    a. Color Saturation
    b. Color Tone
    c. Recolor
6. You can also make adjustments under the **Artistic Effects** tab.

Chapter 12 Themes and Designs

You can get additional themes from Microsoft. Search Microsoft PowerPoint themes on your Internet browser. Microsoft has lots of themes that are developed by third-party developers that are free to download. Themes are a great way to add color, style and a touch of professionalism to a presentation. You can find themes under the **Design** tab. Themes will be added to every page of the presentation. You can go to individual pages and change the color or add a picture as a background that will make the page different from the theme. Sometimes the title page has a slight different layout of the theme.

Changing and Creating a New Theme

To change the theme colors, do the following:

1. On the **Design** tab, in the **Themes** group, *click* **Colors**, a **Custom** dialog drop down window opens.
2. Move your mouse over the different color palettes and your presentation changes to match the color palette.
3. You can also go to the bottom of the **Custom** color drop down window and *click* **Create New Theme Colors**. The **Create New Theme Colors** dialog window opens. The colors inside the **Colors** button represent the theme applied to your presentation.
4. Under **Theme colors**, *click* the drop down buttons next to the name of the theme color element that you want to change.
5. Under **Theme Colors**, do one of the following:

   a. *Click* the down arrow of the color that you want to change, and then choose a color from the main list.
   b. *Click* **More Colors**, and do one of the following:
      i. On the **Standard** tab, select a color.
      ii. On the **Custom** tab, enter a recipe for a color that you want.
6. These steps can be done for all of the theme color elements that you want to change.
7. In the **Name** box, type an appropriate name for the new theme colors, and then *click* **Save**.
8. If you want to return all theme color elements to their original theme colors, *click* **Reset** before you click **Save**.

Change Background Style

You can alter the look of the theme by changing the background style. By changing the background style you may be able to give the background a gradient appeal, change color, or make the background white or black.

1. *Click* **Design** tab.
2. Under the **Background** group, *click* **Background Styles**. Then do one of the following:
   a. *Click* on a background from one of the examples.
   b. *Click* on **Format Background**. The **Format Background** dialog window opens.

i. You can change the gradient color, add a solid color or change to a picture.

Saving Themes

By making changes to the colors, fonts, or line and fill effects of an existing theme, you have designed a theme that fits your special design needs. You should save the changes that you made so that you can apply it to other documents or presentations.

1. *Click* on the **Design** tab.
2. In the **Themes** group, *click* the **More** drop down arrow.
3. *Click* **Save Current Theme**. The **Save Current Theme** file window opens.
4. In the **File name** box, type an appropriate name for the theme, and then *click* **Save**.
5. The revised theme is saved as a .thmx file in the Document Themes folder on your local drive and it is automatically added to the list of custom themes on the **Design** tab in the **Themes** group.

Chapter 13 Transitions

Transitions help for a smooth flow form one slide to another during a slide show. The best way to put transitions between the slides is in the **Slide Sorter** view. *Click* on the **View** tab, and then *click* on the **Slide Sorter** tab under the **Presentation Views** group.

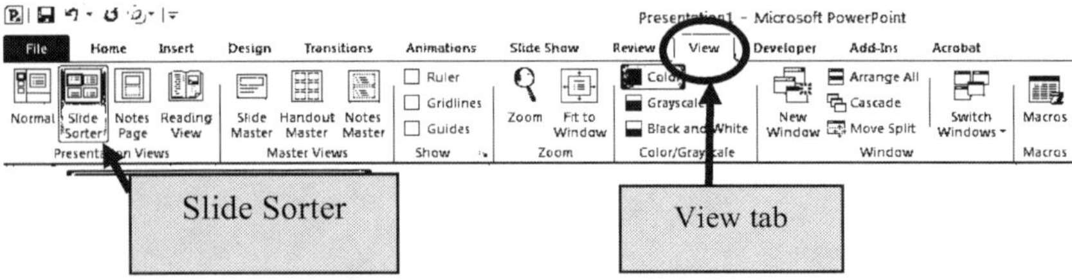

To apply transitions to the presentation follow these steps:

1. *Click* on the **Transition** tab.
2. Under the **Transition to This Slide** group either select a transition or *click* on the **More** drop down arrow to the right of the transition examples.
3. *Click* on the transition you want.
4. The transition will be added to the slide, and a small transition icon will be at the lower left corner of the slide.

You can change some of the transition effects, such as the direction of a Wipe transition. To change the transitions effects,

1. *Click* on the slide that has the transition that you would like to alter.
2. *Click* on the **Transitions** tab.

3. Then *click* on **Effect Options** tab under the **Transition to This Slide** group.

To apply the transition to all the slides *Shift-Click* or *Ctrl-Click* all the slides so they are all selected. Then select the transition from the Transition tab. The transition will be applied to all the slides.

Adding Sound to Transitions

If you would like to add a sound when proceeding from one slide to another follow these steps.

1. *Click* on the slide that you would like to add sound to. The sound will be added to the beginning of the slide.
2. *Click* on the **Transitions** tab.
3. Under the **Timing** group, *click* on the drop down box next to **Sound**.
4. Select the sound that you would like to have while the slide opens.
5. Below the **Sound** drop down box is the **Duration time** box. Use the up or down arrows to increase or decrease the length of time that the sound plays.
6. If you would like to add the sound to every slide, *click* the **Apply to All** tab.

It is better to use only one or two different transitions during a presentation. Too many different transitions may disturb your message, making the audience wonder what transition will be next, instead of listening to your message.

Chapter 14 Working with other Files

Adding Slides from other Presentations

You can add one or more slides to your presentation from another presentation, without having to open the other file. To add slides from files that are located on your computer or on a shared network, do the following:

1. Open the presentation that you want to add a slide to.
2. In the left side pane that contains the **Outline/Slides** tabs, *click* **Slides**, and then *click* between the two slides where you want to add the new slide. A black line will appear and start to flash.
3. On the **Home** tab, in the **Slides** group, *click* the arrow below **New Slide.**
4. *Click* **Reuse Slides**.
5. In the **Reuse Slides** pane, *click* **Open a PowerPoint File**.
6. In the **Browse** dialog box, locate and *click* the presentation file that contains the slide that you want, and then *click* **Open**.
7. After awhile the **Reuse Slides** pane opens, PowerPoint displays thumbnails of the slides from the presentation that you selected. Move your mouse over the slide you want to look at and a larger version of the slide appears.
8. *Click* the slide.

9. To add all of the slides, *right-click* any slide, and then click **Insert All Slides** on the shortcut menu.

Adding Objects from Other Programs

You can insert content or objects from other programs into a Microsoft PowerPoint 2010 presentation. This includes files created by other Microsoft Office programs, as well as files from other programs that support Object Linking and Embedding (OLE). You can insert content only from programs that support OLE and are installed on your computer.

A Linked Object is updated if its source file is changed. For example, a linked chart built from data in Microsoft Excel is changed if the source Excel data changes. The source file must be available on your computer or network to maintain the link between the inserted object and the source data. Inserting a linked object is recommended if the source data set is large or complex. If one of the files is moved the link may be broken, therefore the link will not work.

An Embedded Objects is when the source data is embedded in the presentation. You can view the embedded object on another computer, because the source data is part of the presentation file. Embedded objects typically require more disk space than linked objects. If the source data is changed the embedded object needs to be manually updated.

Insert a Linked Object

When you link a file to a presentation, it can only be opened during the slide show view. You will have to move the mouse over the object and *click* on the object to open the linked file.

1. *Click* in the slide where you want to place the object.
2. On the **Insert** tab, in the **Text** group, *click* **Object**.
3. An **Inset Object** dialog window opens. *Click* **Create from File** option box.
4. In the **File** box, type the name of the file, or *click* **Browse** to select from a list.
5. Select the **Link** check box.
6. Do one of the following:

- To display the content in your presentation, clear the **Display as Icon** check box.
- To display an icon that is *clicked* to view the object, select the **Display as Icon** check box.
- To change the default icon image or label, *click* **Change Icon**, and then *click* the icon that you want from the **Icon** list. If you want, you can type a label in the **Caption** box.

Insert an Embedded Object

1. *Click* on the slide where you want to place the object.
2. On the **Insert** tab, in the **Text** group, *click* **Object**.
3. Do one of the following:

- To create a new object, *click* **Create New**. In the **Object type** box, *click* the type of object that you want to create.

- If the object already exists, *click* **Create From File**. In the **File** box, type the name of the file, or *click* **Browse** to select from a file list.

4. Clear the **Link** check box.
5. Do one of the following:

- To display the content in your presentation, clear the **Display as Icon** check box.
- To display an icon that is *clicked* to view the object, select the **Display as Icon** check box.

To change the default icon image or label, *click* **Change Icon**, and then *click* the icon that you want from the **Icon** list. If you want, you can type a label in the **Caption** box.

Link or embed content copied from another program

In a program other than PowerPoint, you can select and copy the information that you want to insert as an object.

1. Go to the program that has the information you would like to copy.
2. Highlight the information and *click* **Copy**.
3. In PowerPoint, *click* on the page where you want the object to appear.
4. On the **Home** tab, in the **Clipboard** group, *click* the arrow below **Paste**.
5. In the **Paste Options** dialog box, do one of the following:

- Use Destination Theme
- Keep Source Formatting
- Picture

- Keep Text Only

6. Or you can *click* Paste Special. In the **Paste Special** dialog box, do one of the following:

- **Paste**. The **Paste** option button lets you paste as HTML, Drawing Object, Picture, Bitmap, or text.
- **Paste Link**. To paste the information as a linked object, *click* **Paste link**.

Chapter 15 Templates

Using templates is a great way to give your presentation a consistent look throughout the slide show. Some template options are:

- Template Colors can be consistent throughout the presentation.
- Pictures and text can have placeholders for easy replacement.
- Change the colors within the theme. *Click* the **Design** tab, in the **Themes** group, and then *click* on the **Colors** tab. (This is not available to all templates).
- Fonts, tiles and placements for text and pictures are consistent every time you use the template.

Apply a Template

When you want your presentation to contain thoughtful arrangement of elements and color, fonts, effects, style, and layout to your plain slides, apply a template. This will give you a jump-start on a new, blank presentation.

Templates can be created by you, downloaded from Microsoft Office.com or downloaded from third-party's Web site. To download templates from Microsoft Office.com, see the options available from the PowerPoint Template categories on Office.com.

To apply a template, do the following:

1. On the **File** tab, *click* **New**.
2. Under **Available Templates and Themes**, do one of the following:

- To reuse a template that you've recently used, *click* **Recent Templates**.
- To use a template that you installed to your local drive previously, *click* **My Templates**, *click* the template that you want, and then *click* **OK**.
- Under **Office.com Templates,** *click* a template category, select a template, and then *click* **Download** to download the template from Office.com to your local drive.

You should start developing a template in the **Slide Master** View.

1. In the **View** tab, *click* on **Slide Master** in the **Master Views** group.
2. Make the changes to the slides in the **Master View** using the **Insert Placeholder**, **Title**, **Footer** and other insert tabs.
3. Click on the **File** tab.
4. Click on **Save As**.
5. Give the template file a name.
6. In the drop down box **Save as Type**, select **PowerPoint Template**.

Saving a Template

When you create a presentation, and want to be able to use the template again, then you need to save it as a PowerPoint Template (.potx) file. Under the POTX format you can share it with your colleagues and reuse it more than once.

On the **File** tab, *click* **Save As**, in the File name box, name your template, and then in the Save as type box, select **PowerPoint Template (*.POTX).**

Chapter 16 Creating Sections

1. Add a Section

Click the slide thumbnail where you want to begin a new section. Under the **Home** tab, **Slides** category, *click* the **Section** drop down menu > **Add Section**. An Untitled Section name header will appear in the Navigation Pane on the right.

2. Name a Section

Right-click on Untitled Section header. Select **Rename Section**.

3. Section Sequencing

Other than naming each section, the sequence that you choose may be the most important step you can take in preparing your sales presentation. The Section names will help determine what content – which should be different for each event – needs to be researched and included in each presentation. Here are some ideas for section names.

Section One – Title Slide

This slide should reflect your branding efforts. This should match your website, business cards and other advertising color and mood. The title slide should also tell the audience problems you are going to solve or highlight.

If you were giving a presentation for a job interview, this section would have your name and the position that you are applying for.

Section Two – Agenda Slide

Tell the audience what you're going to cover. Many times this slide is a list of what subjects will be covered. For most presentations this will list only three topics.

For employment, this would list your top three achievements.

Section Three – History of Problem

This can be a single statement or can be broken down into how the problem started, what the costs are, and what will happen if the problem is not solved. Do your homework on the audience, and create slides that emphasize potential issues in their industry. Show that you understand your audience's specific "pain".

For employment this would explain the problems that existed that you found or worked on.

Section Four - Approach / Philosophy

Do not talk about yourself. Talk about the solution that you bring. This is when they will see that you not only understand their pain, but you have solutions. Don't give the details of the solutions; most likely you are trying to get hired as a consultant or as an employee. If you tell them the details of the solution, they don't need you anymore. Remember, a good consultant knows how to keep the income stream running. This is where you can demonstrate how much better your audience's life will be with your solution. Graphics are particularly helpful here.

Case studies and stories of past clients or projects are a great way to bring this home.

For employment, this would explain the process you used to solve the problem.

Section Five – Products / Services

If you are selling an item or you are a consultant this Section should be short but to the point. Relate your product or service to their needs, showing them the benefits.

For employment, this section would tell the benefits that were the results of your solution on the project; time savings, money saved and/or other benefits.

Section Six – Summary

Now, tie everything you've just said together. This is your final opportunity to remind your audience of how your product/service will make their lives better. If there is one thought you'd like them to walk away with, this is your chance.

For employment, this would highlight how you can solve their problems using the skills and experiences that you have from solving other problems.

Section Seven – Call to Action

This is your call to action section. Make the proposed action measurable and accountable by assigning dates and leaders. A graphic timeline is very helpful here.

For employment, you could layout a 30, 60 & 90 day plan on how you will move forward in the position once you are hired.

Section Eight – Thank you Slide

The closing slide displays as you thank your audience for their time. People still like to write things down, so including your name and contact information here will be useful.

1 Keep it simple – the attention should be on you, not your PowerPoint presentation.

2 Use objects like pictures or shapes instead of bullet points and limit the number. The audience should be listening to you not be reading the presentation.

3 When you use bullet points, be creative with symbols or pictures as bullet points.

4 Do not give handouts prior to the presentation. The audience will be reading instead of listening.
5 Limit transitions and animations.
6 It is better to have a personalized theme than PowerPoint Templates.
7 Use appropriate charts and design. Charts and artworks should have meaning in your story.
8 Use color well.
9 Use readable fonts. Color, size and background should be pleasing to the eyes.
10 Fonts should be readable from the back of the room, use a fonts of 28 or larger.
11 Use sound and videos wisely.
12 Make sure slides flow from slide to slide.
13 Never run over your allowed time. The audience will be upset and forget your message or they will have negative feelings about you and your product.

Chapter 17 Sound (Audio)

Apply Sound Effects

You can give additional emphasis to animated text or objects by applying sound effects.

To add sound to animated text or an object, do the following:

1 Select the object that you want to animate.

2 *Click* the **Animations** tab.

3 In the **Advanced Animation** group, *click* **Animation Pane**. The **Animation Pane** opens on the right side of the workspace pane, showing the order, type and duration of animation effects applied to text or objects on a slide.

4 Locate the effect to which you want to add sound, *click* the down arrow and then *click* **Effect Options**. A windows dialog opens.

5 On the **Effect** tab, under **Enhancements**, in the **Sound** box, *click* the arrow to open the list and then do one of the following:

- *Click* a sound from the list, and then *click* **OK**.
- To add a sound from a file, *click* **Other Sound, (at the bottom of the list)** and then locate the sound file that you want to use. *Click* **OK**. When you *click* **OK**, the slide plays a preview of the animation with the sound added.

a. To change the preview sound volume, *click* **Sound Icon** in the dialog window and move the slider up or down. To turn off the preview sound, select the **Mute** check box.

6 To preview the animations and sounds applied to a slide, *click* **Play** in the **Animation Pane**.

Adding and Playing Sounds

To add a mood to your presentation you can add audio, such as music, narration, or sound bites. When you insert an audio clip on a slide, a sound icon appears that represents the audio file. While you give your presentation, you can set the audio clip to play automatically when the slide displays, to start when you *click* the mouse, or to play across all slides in the presentation, and controlling it to continue by looping until you stop it. You can add an audio clip from files on your computer, a network, or the **Clip Art** task pane. You can also record your own audio to add to a presentation or use music from a CD. You can preview an audio clip and you can hide the audio icon during a slide show.

Add an Audio Clip

To prevent playback issues, you can embed your audio clips in your presentation.

1 *Click* the slide to which you want to add an audio clip.

2 On the **Insert** tab, in the **Media** group, *click* **Audio**.

3 Do one of the following:

- *Click* **Audio from File**, then locate the folder that contains the file, and then *double-click* the file that you want to add.

- *Click* **Clip Art Audio**, and then locate the audio clip that you want in the **Clip Art** task pane, and then *double-click* to add it to the slide.
- *Click* **Record Audio**. A **Record Sound** dialog windows appears that lets you record a sound or voice. *Click* the **red dot** button to record.

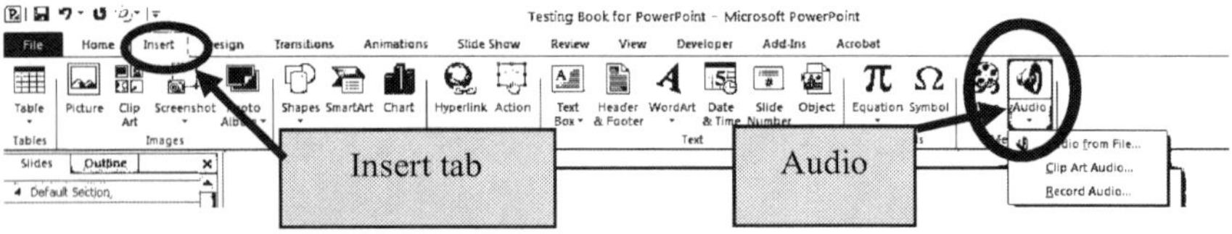

Preview an Audio Clip

You can preview an audio clip before adding it to your presentation.

1 *Click* on the object you are adding sound.

2 *Click* the **Insert** tab.

3 *Click* on the drop down arrow on the **Audio** tab in the **Media** group.

4 *Click* on **Clip Art Audio**.

5 The **Clip Art** search pane opens.

6 In the **Clip Art** task pane, in the box that displays the available clips, *click* the down arrow on the right side of the Audio example box.

7 *Click* **Preview/Properties**.

8 When the **Preview/Properties** dialog box opens the audio should play, if the audio does not automatically plays *click* the **Play** arrow button.

Preview an audio clip on a slide

If an object or a slide already has audio you can preview the sound by following these steps.

1 *Click* on the **Audio Clip** icon. An audio slide will appear.
2 Below the icon, *click* the **Play** button. The Play button is the far left arrow button on the slide.

Set the playback options for an audio clip

1 On the slide, select the audio clip icon.
2 Under **Audio Tools - Playback** tab, in the **Audio Options** group, do one of the following:

- To start the audio clip automatically, *click* **Audio Tools – Playback**. In the **Audio Option** group *click* on the drop down arrow next to the **Start** list, *click* **Automatically**.
- To manually start the audio clip, *click* **Audio Tools – Playback**. In the **Audio Option** group, click on the drop down arrow next to the **Start** list, *click* **On Click.**
- To play an audio clip as you *click* through the slides in your presentation, *click* **Audio Tools – Playback**. In the **Audio Option** group, *click* on the drop down arrow next to the **Start** list, *click* **Play across slides**.
- To play an audio clip continuously until you stop it, select the **Loop Until Stopped** check box in the **Audio Options** group under the **Audio Tools –**

Playback tab. When you loop a sound, it plays continuously until you advance to the next slide.

If you add multiple audio clips, they will appear on top of each other, and each will play in the order in which they were added. If you want each audio clip to start when you *click* it, *drag* the audio clip icons off of each other after you insert them.

Hide the Audio Clip Icon

Use this option only if you set the audio clip to play automatically, or if you created some other kind of control, such as a trigger to *click* to play the clip. (A trigger is something on your slide, such as a picture, shape, button, paragraph of text, or text box, that can set off an action when you click it.)

1 *Click* the audio clip icon.

2 Under **Audio Tools - Playback** tab, in the **Audio Options** group, select the **Hide During Show** check box.

Add or Remove Bookmarks

You can add bookmarks to indicate time points of interest in a video or audio clip. Use bookmarks as a way to trigger animations or to jump to a specific location in a video. Bookmarks are useful when delivering a presentation; you can use them to help you find specific points in a video (or audio clip) quickly.

Add a bookmark

1 Insert a video or audio clip to a slide.

2 In the audio or video controls below the audio or video clip, press play (arrow on the far left of the control panel). As the audio or video plays, look for the point where you want to start the bookmark. **Pause** the audio or video.

3 To indicate a point of interest, do one of the following:

- If you are working with a video clip, under **Video Tools - Playback** tab, in the **Bookmarks** group, *click* **Add Bookmark**. A small yellow dot will appear on the progression bar.
- If you are working with an audio clip, under **Audio Tools**, on the **Playback** tab, in the **Bookmarks** group, *click* **Add Bookmark**. A small yellow dot will appear on the progression bar.

4 To shorten your clip, use the **Trim video** or **Trim audio** buttons.

a. *Click* on the video or audio that you would like to shorten.

b. *Click* on the **Video Tools – Playback** tab or **Audio Tools – Playback** tab.

c. *Click* on the **Trim Video** or **Trim Audio** button in the **Editing** group.

d. The **Trim Video** or **Trim Audio** dialog window will open.

e. Move the **green** bar right to where you would like the video or audio to start.

f. Move the **red** bar left to where you would like the video or audio to stop.

g. *Click* **OK**.

Remove a bookmark

1 In the time line, locate and *click* the bookmark that you want to remove.

2 Do one of the following:

- If you are working with a video clip, under **Video Tools**, on the **Playback** tab, in the **Bookmarks** group, *click* **Remove Bookmark.**
- If you are working with an audio clip, under **Audio Tools**, on the **Playback** tab, in the **Bookmarks** group, *click* **Remove Bookmark**.

Compress Media Files

You can improve playback performance and save disk space by compressing your media files.

1 Open the presentation that contains the audio or video files.

2 On the **File** tab, *click* **Info**, and then in the **Media Size and Performance** section, *click* **Compress Media**.

3 To specify the quality of the video or audio, which in turn, determines the size of the video or audio, select one of the following:

- **Presentation Quality** - Save space while maintaining overall audio and video quality.
- **Internet Quality -** Quality will be comparable to media that is streamed over the Internet.
- **Low Quality** - Use when space is limited, such as when you are sending presentations via e-mail.

To get a higher quality of audio use an USB microphone.

Delete Audio Clips

To delete an audio clips, do the following:

1 Locate the slide that contains the audio clip that you want to delete.

2 In **Normal** view, *click* the **Sound Icon** or **CD icon**, and then press **Delete**.

Optimize Media for Compatibility

The **Optimize Compatibility** command in PowerPoint will help you to resolve playback issues. To avoid playback issues when your PowerPoint presentation contains media, such as video or audio files, you can optimize the media files for compatibility. This makes it easy to share your presentation with others or take it with you to another location (perhaps to use a different computer to present it elsewhere) and your slideshow will play correctly.

1 When you are ready to share your presentation, with the presentation open in PowerPoint, on the **File** tab, *click* **Info**.

2 If the media in your presentation was inserted in a format that could present compatibility issues when played on another computer, the **Optimize Compatibility** option will appear.

3 When the **Optimize Compatibility** appears, it provides a summarization for resolutions of potential playback issues. It also provides a list of the number of occurrences of media in the presentation. The following are common scenarios that can cause playback issues:

- If you have linked videos, the **Optimize for Compatibility** summarization will report that you need to embed them. *Click* the **View Links** option to proceed. Thc dialog box that opens will allow you to embed the videos simply by *clicking* **Break Link** for each media item that you want to embed.
- If you have videos that were inserted using an earlier version of PowerPoint, such as version 2007, you will need to upgrade your media file format in order to ensure that these files will play back. Upgrading will automatically update and embed these media items to the new format. Once you have upgraded, you should run the **Optimize for Compatibility** command.
- To upgrade your media files from an earlier version to PowerPoint 2010 (and if the files were linked, they will be embedded), on the **File** tab, *click* **Info**, and then *click* **Convert**.

Media Trouble

If you are having trouble playing or inserting media, it is likely that you do not have the proper codec installed. For example, if you wanted to send someone a PowerPoint presentation with media already inserted, and that media is based on a codec that the may not have installed. The best solution is for you to run **Optimize Compatibility** *before* sending the file. Try one of the following to help resolve any lingering issues:

- One solution is to download a third-party media decoder and encoder filter, which will allow you to decode and encode a variety of formats.
- If you decide to deliver the presentation that you created on a PC, on an Apple Macintosh, the file formats, WMV and WMA are not native to a Macintosh computer. In this case you will need an Internet connection so that you can download a QuickTime component (for the Mac operating system) that supports Windows Media Video, to play these your media files.

Trim Audio Clips

You can trim audio at the beginning and end of each clip. Perhaps, a narration discusses a subject that is not pertinent to the message of your audio clip or you want to shorten the audio to fit with the timing of your slides.

1 Select the audio clip, and then press **Play**.

2 Select the video on the slide.

3 Under **Audio Tools - Playback** tab, in the **Editing** group, *click* **Trim Audio**.

4 In the **Trim Audio** dialog box, do one or more of the following:

- To trim the beginning of the clip, *click* the start point (shown in the image below as a **green** marker, on the far left). When you see the two-headed arrow, *drag* the arrow to the desired starting position for the audio clip.
- To trim the end of the clip, *click* the end point (shown in the image below as a red marker, on the right). When you see the two-headed arrow, *drag* the arrow to the desired ending position for the audio clip.

Add Audio to Hyperlinks

Select the hyperlink to which you want to add a sound effect.

1 On the **Insert** tab, in the **Links** group, *click* **Action.**

2 Do one of the following:

- To apply the sound effect when the hyperlink is clicked, *click* the **Mouse Click** tab.
- To apply the sound effect when the pointer rests on the hyperlink, *click* the **Mouse Over** tab.

3 Select the **Play sound** check box, and then *click* the sound that you want to play.

Record and add Narration & Timings

Audio narrations and timings can enhance a Web-based or self-running slide show. If you're planning to create a video with your presentation, using narrations and timings is a great way to bring excitement to your presentation. You can use audio narration to archive a meeting, so that presenters or absentees can review the presentation later and hear any comments made during the presentation.

You can also record your use of the laser pointer in the slide show together with your narrations during a show.

You can either record a narration before you run a slide show or record a narration during a slide show and include audience comments in the recording. If you don't want narration throughout the presentation, you can record comments only on selected slides or turn off the narration so that it plays only when you want it to play.

When you add a narration to a slide, a sound icon appears on the slide. As with any sound, you can either *click* the icon to play the sound or set the sound to play automatically. To record and hear a narration, your computer must be equipped with a sound card, microphone, and speakers.

Record Narrations

1 When you record a narration, you run through the presentation and record each slide. You can pause and resume recording any time.

2 Ensure your microphone is set up and in working order prior to recording your slide show.

3 On the **Slide Show** tab, in the **Set Up** group, *click* **Record Slide Show** drop down arrow.

4 Select one of the following:

- **Start Recording from Beginning**
- **Start Recording from Current Slide**

5 In the **Record Slide Show** dialog box, select the **Narrations and laser pointer** check box, and if appropriate, select or deselect the **Slide and animation timings** check box.

6 *Click* **Start Recording**.

7 To pause the narration, *click* **Pause** in the **Recording** dialog menu.

8 To resume your narration, *click* **Resume Recording**.

9 To end your slide show recording, *right-click* the slide, and then *click* **End Show**. You can also hit the *Esc* key.

10 The recorded slide show timings are automatically saved and the slide show appears in **Slide Sorter** view with timings beneath each slide.

Preview a Narration

1 In **Normal** view, on the slide, *click* the **sound icon**.

2 On the ribbon, under **Audio Tools**, on the **Playback** tab, in the **Preview** group, *click* **Play.**

Record Comments

1 In **Normal** view, *click* the slide that you want to add a comment to.

2. On the **Insert** tab, in the **Media** group, *click* the arrow under **Audio**, and then *click* **Record Audio.**
3. To record the comment, *click* the **Record** button (red round button), and start speaking.
4. When you are finished recording, click **Stop** button. (The blue square button).
5. In the **Name** box, type a name for the sound, and then *click* **OK**.
6. A sound icon appears on the slide.

Turn Off or Delete Narrations

Turning off the narration does not delete the narration from your presentation — it only prevents the narration from playing. Deleting the narration permanently removes it from your presentation.

To turn off the narration do one of the following:

- On the **Slide Show** tab, in the **Set Up** group, clear the **Play Narrations** check box.
- You can also *click* **Set Up Slide Show**, and under **Show Options** select the **Show Without Narration** check box.

To turn the narration back on, ensure the **Show without narration** check box is cleared and the **Play Narrations** check box is selected.

To delete the narration

Narration is deleted on each slide individually, in **Normal** view – on the **View** tab, in the **Presentation Views** group, *click* **Normal**. Each slide with narration has a sound indicator on a lower corner.

1 *Click* the **sound indicator** and then press **Delete**.
2 Repeat step 1 for each slide from which you want to delete the narration.

Automatically Play Audio Files

Follow this procedure to play an audio file automatically when you introduce a slide. You can delay the playtime by any amount of time, so it appears that it is playing automatically.

1 Select the **audio icon** on the slide.
2 On the **Animations** tab, in the **Advanced Animation** group, *click* the **Add Animation** button.
3 Under **Media**, select **Play**.
4 To display the **Animation** pane, in the **Advanced Animation** group, *click* **Animation Pane**.
5 In the **Animation Pane**, *click* the arrow to the right of the animation, and then *click* **Effect Options**.
6 On the **Effect** tab under **Start Playing**, select **From Beginning**.
7 Under **Stop Playing**, select **After Current Slide**.
8 On the **Timing** tab, in the **Start** list, select **With Previous**.
9 In the **Delay** box, press the up arrow up or down to start the audio file the delayed time that you would like.
10 *Click* **OK**.
11 To preview and test this, on the **Slide Show** tab, in the **Start Slide show** group, *click* **From Beginning**.

Preview the time to make sure that the time delay is set right.

Turn off or hide media controls in Slide Show view

Other than *clicking* away from the media (audio/video), control bar, you can turn off or hide the media control bar while in Slide Show view by doing the following:

1. On the **Slide Show** tab, in the **Set Up** group, deselect the **Show Media Controls** check box.
2. The media control bar is visible in **Slide Show** view when you mouse over it.

Chapter 18 Videos

Adding and Playing a Video

You can link an external video or GIF animation file to your Microsoft PowerPoint 2010 presentation. By linking your video, you can reduce the file size of your presentation. You can also embed a video in your presentation, which can help to eliminate issues with missing files and other linking problems. You can use both video and animated GIF files from the Clip Art library. I found that the video files that work best are MOV files or M4V, but PowerPoint will support MP4, MOV, AVI, and SWF files when you have installed the right media players such as QuickTime and Adobe Flash players.

There are some limitations when using Flash in PowerPoint 2010, including the inability to use special effects (such as shadows, reflections, glow effects, soft edges, bevels, and 3-D rotation), the fade and trim capabilities, and the ability to compress these files for easier sharing and distribution.

PowerPoint 2010 64-bit is not compatible with 32-bit versions of QuickTime or Flash. You must install a 64-bit version of QuickTime or Flash, or a 32-bit version of PowerPoint 2010.

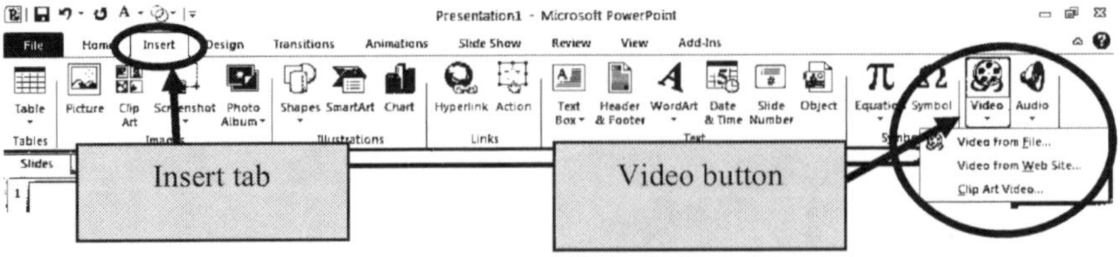

To embed a video from your PowerPoint presentation, do the following:

1. On the **Slides** tab in **Normal** view (on the left side of the window), *click* the slide to which you want to add a video or animated GIF file.
2. On the **Insert** tab, in the **Media** group, *click* the arrow under **Video**. Note: if you are on a new slide there may be an **Insert Media Clip** icon in the text box. You can *click* on the icon.

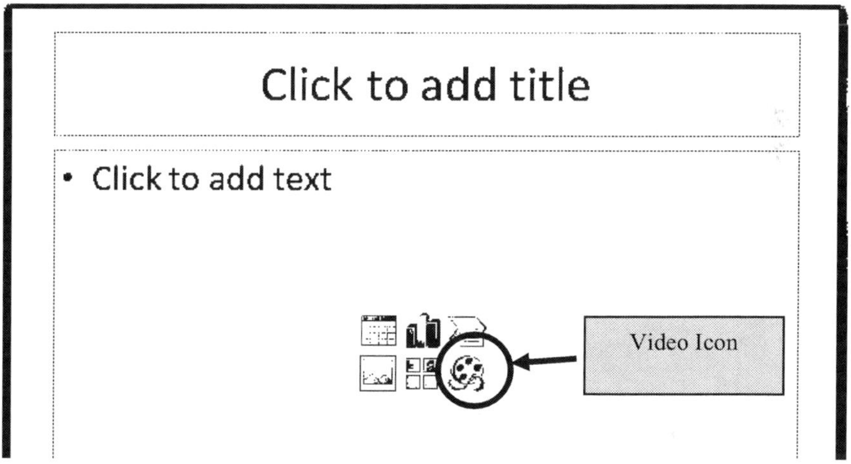

3. *Click* **Video from File**, locate and *click* the file that you want to link to.
4. *Click* **Insert**. This will embed the video.
    a. To link a file: On the **Insert** button, *click* the down arrow, and then *click* **Link to file**. To prevent possible problems with broken links, it is a good idea to copy the video into the same folder as your presentation, and link to them there.

To link to a video into your PowerPoint presentation, do the following:

1. Insert text, a shape or some object that you can *click* on during a slide show. *Click* on the object.
2. *Click* on the **Insert** tab.
3. *Click* on **Hyperlink**.
4. Find the video file that you want to link to. *Click* on the file.
5. *Click* **OK**.

During the slide show, the mouse cursor may not be able to *click* on the object. In this case, hit the **Tab** key (which will highlight the first link), and then hit the **Enter** key.

Embed an Animated GIF

PowerPoint comes with a good selection of clip art and some of the clip art are animated. Mostly it is hard to tell if the clip art is animated or not, until you see them in the slide show. To determine what type of file the clip art is, move your mouse over the clip art in the clip art search pane. Or click on the drop down arrow on the right side of the clip are (in the Clip Art search pane). Then *click* on **Preview Properties**. The Type is shown in the **Preview Properties** dialog window. The GIF files are the only file type that can be animated.

1. In **Normal** view, *click* the slide in which you want to embed an animated GIF file.
2. On the **Insert** tab, in the **Media** group, *click* the arrow under **Video**, and then *click* **Clip Art Video**.
3. The **Clip Art** search pane opens, in the **Search for** box, enter the key word that describes the selection of animated GIFs that you want to preview. Or you

can search through the animated clip art by scrolling through the list.

4. In the **Results should be** box, "Selected media file types". Ensure that only the **Videos** check box is selected.
5. *Click* **Go**.
6. Once you find the Clip Art animated file *click* on it. The Clip Art file is now on the presentation. During the slide show the clip art file will be animated like a video.

Background Videos

Now that you can embed videos in your presentations, you may want to use one of your videos as a background for your slides.

To embed from a file and use it as a background on a slide, do the following:

1. In **Normal** view, *click* the slide in which you want to embed a video.
2. On the **Insert** tab, in the **Media** group, *click* the arrow under **Video**, and then *click* **Video from file**.
3. In the **Insert Video** dialog box, locate and *click* the video that you want to embed, and then *click* **Insert**.
4. On the slide, select the corner sizing handles of the video frame, and then *drag* each so that you cover the slide with the video frame. Depending on the

video you may distort the video if you drag one part of the video that changes the video ratio format.

5. Under **Video Tools – Format** tab, under the **Arrange** group, *click* on **Send Backwards** arrow and select **Send to Back**. If the **Video Tools – Format** tab is not visible, make sure that the video is selected.
6. If you are going to have text, shapes, or pictures on top of the video it might be a good thing to fade the video, making it easier to view the text or picture.
7. To fade the video follow these steps:
    a. Make sure the video is selected. In the **Video Tools – Format** tab, *click* **Corrections** button.
    b. Select the fade level you would like.
    c. You can do further adjustments under the **Video Correction Options** (at the bottom of the **Correction – Brightness and Contrast** popup window.

Turn Off or Hide Media Controls

Other than clicking away from the media (audio/video) control bar, you can turn off or hide the media control bar while in **Slide Show** view by doing the following:

1. On the **Slide Show** tab, in the **Set Up** group, deselect the **Show Media Controls** check box.
2. The media control bar is visible in **Slide Show** view when you mouse over it. Sometimes when you *click*

the video control bar during the slide show, the slide show will advance to the next slide instead of playing the video.

3. This could be caused by several things, check the following list to trouble shoot the cause:

- Make sure you are not presenting a recorded vision of PowerPoint presentation.
- Make sure that under **Set Up Slide Show** that the **Show Type – Presented by a Speaker (Full Screen)** is selected.

Sometimes the **Use Timing** option under **Slide Show** tab can also cause problems, so you might have to uncheck this option.

Linking a Video

You can link to a video file on your local drive or to a video file that is on a social media web site, such as YouTube.

1. On the **Slides** tab in **Normal** view, *click* the slide to which you want to add a video.
2. In your browser, go to the web site that contains the video that you want to link to, such as YouTube.
3. On the web site, locate the video, and then locate and copy the **Embed** code. Most social media video web sites include an embed code. Some web sites will not have an embed code, and therefore you

cannot link to those. You might have to *right-click* on the video to find **Copy Embed HTML**.

4. Back in PowerPoint, on the **Insert** tab, in the **Media** group, *click* the arrow under **Video**.
5. *Click* **Video From Web Site**.
6. In the **Video From Web Site** dialog box, paste the embed code, and then *click* **Insert**. You may have to resize the embed code box.

Add or Remove Bookmarks

You can add bookmarks to the time line to indicate points of interest in a video or audio clip. Use bookmarks as a way to trigger animations or to jump to a specific location in a video.

While delivering a presentation bookmarks can you find specific points in a video (or audio clip) quickly.

Add a bookmark

1. Insert a video or audio clip to a slide.
2. In the audio or video controls below the audio or video clip, press **Play** (arrow on the far left of the control panel). As the audio or video plays, look for points of interest.
3. To indicate a point of interest, do one of the following:

- If you are working with a video clip, under **Video Tools - Playback** tab, in the **Bookmarks** group, *click* **Add Bookmark**.

- If you are working with an audio clip, under **Audio Tools - Playback** tab, in the **Bookmarks** group, *click* **Add Bookmark**.

Remove a bookmark

1. In the time line, locate and *click* the bookmark that you want to remove.
2. Do one of the following:

- If you are working with a video clip, under **Video Tools - Playback** tab, in the **Bookmarks** group, *click* **Remove Bookmark**.
- If you are working with an audio clip, under **Audio Tools - Playback** tab, in the **Bookmarks** group, *click* **Remove Bookmark**.

Trim a Video

After you watch your video clips, you might notice that the beginning of the video or the end of the video has excess video that you do not want to show and you would like to remove these parts. You can cut out beginning or ending parts of your video with the **Trim Video**.

1. Select the video on the slide.
2. *Click* on **Video Tools – Playback** tab.
3. Under **Video Tools - Playback** tab, in the **Editing** group, *click* **Trim Video**.
4. In the **Trim Video** dialog box, do one or more of the following:

- To trim the beginning of the clip, *click* the start point (shown in the image below as a green marker, on the far left). When you see the two-headed arrow, *drag* the arrow to the desired starting position for the video.

- To trim the end of the clip, *click* the end point (shown in the image below as a red marker, on the right). When you see the two-headed arrow, *drag* the arrow to the desired ending position for the video.

5. *Click* **OK**

Applying Special Effects to Videos

You can apply shadows, reflections, glow effects, soft edges, bevels, and 3-D rotation to a video.

1. *Click* the video on the slide that you want to add an effect to.
2. Under **Video Tools - Format** tab, in the **Video Styles** group, *click* **Video Effects**.
3. If you do not see the **Video Tools - Format** tab, *double-click* the video to make sure that you have selected it.
4. Do one or more of the following:
   a. To apply or change a preset combination of effects, point to **Preset**, and then *click* the effect that you want. The **Preset** is broken into three areas:
      1) No Preset
      2) Presets

3) **3-D Options**, this option brings up the Format Video dialog window where you can make changes to the video, such as:
   - Border Color
   - Border Style
   - Shadow
   - Reflection
   - Glow and Soft Edges
   - 3-D Format
   - 3-D Rotation
   - Video
   - Crop
   - Size
   - Position
   - Alt Text

b. To apply or change a shadow, point to **Shadow**, and then *click* the shadow that you want.
   - No Shadow
   - Outer
   - Inner
   - Perspective
   - **Shadow Options**, this option brings up the Format Video dialog window where you can make changes to the video.

c. To apply or change a reflection, point to **Reflection**, and then *click* the option that you want.
   - No Reflection

- Reflection Variations
- **Reflection Options**, this option brings up the Format Video dialog window where you can make changes to the video.

d. To apply or change a glow, point to **Glow**, and then *click* the glow variation that you want.

- No Glow
- Glow Variations
- More Glow Colors
- Glow Options this option brings up the Format Video dialog window where you can make changes to the video.

e. To apply or change a soft edge, point to **Soft Edges**, and then *click* the size of the edge that you want.

- No Soft Edges
- 1 Point to 50 Points
- **Soft Edges Options** this option brings up the Format Video dialog window where you can make changes to the video.

f. To apply or change an edge, point to **Bevel**, and then *click* the bevel that you want.

- No Bevel
- Bevel
- **3-D Options** this option brings up the Format Video dialog window where you can make changes to the video.

g. To apply or change a 3-D rotation, point to **3-D Rotation**, and then *click* the rotation that you want.
   - No Rotation
   - Parallel
   - Perspective
   - Oblique
   - 3-D Rotation Options this option brings up the Format Video dialog window where you can make changes to the video.

Shaping Videos

You can play your video in a frame shaped like a circle, arrow, star, and a call out, or any other shape that is located in the Video Shapes list. After you apply a shape to your video, you can add a border, special video effects, or recolor your video.

1) Select the video on the slide.
2) Under **Video Tools - Format** tab, in the **Video Styles** group, *click* **Video Shape.**
3) Select the shape that you want your video to play in.

Recolor a Video

You can recolor your video by applying a built-in stylized color effect, such as a sepia tone or grayscale.

1) On the slide, select the video that you want to recolor.
2) Under **Video Tools - Format** tab, in the **Adjust** group, *click* **Color**.
3) Do one or more of the following:

- Choose from the pre-built, stylized **recolor** effects.
- To view additional colors, including variations of theme colors, standard, or custom colors, *click* **More Variations**. The recolor effect will be applied using the color variation. By moving your mouse pointer over the recolor effects you will see the video on the slide change color. If you pick a color use the **Play** button under **Video Tools – Format** tab in the **Preview** group to view the video in the new color. You can change color if you do not like the first color you picked. The first example in the **Recolor** will reset the video to the original video colors.
- **Video Color Options** will open up the **Format Video** dialog window where you can make changes to the video.

Resize a Video Frame

Whether you have a linked or embedded video in your presentation, you can resize or hide it.

When you do not want to play a video at its original resolution, you can resize a video frame on a slide by dragging a corner-sizing handle to increase or decrease the size, or you can specify precise height-to-width proportions.

1) In Normal view, select the video that you want to resize on the slide.
2) Do one of the following:

- To adjust the size of the video on the slide *click* a corner sizing handle until you see a two-headed arrow, and then *drag* to size the frame. To keep the center of the video in the same place, hold down *CTRL* key while dragging. This maintains the proportions of the video as you drag. The standard videos will have a 4:3 aspect ratio, where wide screen and high-definition videos have a 16:9 ratio. If the aspect ratios of the presentation and the video differ, your video will look distorted when it plays.
- To specify precise height-to-width proportions of a video:

a. Under **Video Tools - Format** tab, in the **Size** group, move the up and sown arrows on the **Height and Width** to change the size. You can also *click* on the small **Launcher** button (in the lower right hand corner or the Size group) and you will pull up the **Format Video** dialog window. In the dialog window you can do the following:

b. *Click* **Size**, and then under **Scale**, select the **Lock Aspect Ratio** check box.
c. Under **Size and Rotate**, enter sizes in the **Height** and **Width** boxes. You can also rotate the video in the **Size and Rotate** section.
d. Under **Scale**, in the **Height** and **Width** list boxes, enter the percentage of size that you want, relative to the video's original size.
e. To prevent videos from skipping when they are played, under **Scale**, select the **Best scale for slide show** check box.

Hide a video when it's not playing

If you select the option to hide a video when it is not playing and you have selected the **Play Full Screen** checkbox (Under the **Video Tools – Playback** tab in the **Video Options** group), the video will not appear to be on your slide at all. You should create an automatic or triggered animation to initiate playback or you will never see the video play during the slideshow.

1. In **Normal** view, *click* the video frame on the slide.
2. Under **Video Tools - Playback** tab, in the **Video Options** group, select the **Hide While Not Playing** check box.

Playing a Video

Set this option before adding any animations or triggers to your video. By changing this option, you will remove any animations that are associated with your video.

1. In Normal view, *click* the video frame on the slide.
2. Under **Video Tools - Playback** tab, in the **Video Options** group, in the **Start** list, do one of the following:

- *Click* **Automatically** to play your video when the slide containing the video appears in **Slide Show** view.
- *Click* **On Click** to control when you want to start the video by clicking the mouse. Then in **Slide Show** view, simply *click* the video frame when you are ready to play the video. You can pause a video while it is playing by *clicking* it. To continue playing the video, *click* it again.

Play a video full screen

You can play a video so that it fills the entire slide (screen) when you deliver your presentation. Depending on the resolution of your original video file, it might appear distorted or blurry when you enlarge it. Many times the color has a washed out look. Always preview your video before you include it in your presentation so that if the video appears distorted or blurry, you can undo the full screen option.

1. In **Normal** view, *click* the video frame on the slide that you want to play full screen.

2. Under **Video Tools - Playback** tab, in the **Video Options** group, select the **Play Full Screen** check box.

Preview a video

1. In **Normal** view, *click* the video frame.
2. In **Video Tools – Playback** tab, in the **Preview** group *click* **Play**.
3. You can also *click* the **Play** button on the video (the arrow button on the far left side of the video bar on the bottom of the video.

Set the volume of a video

1. You can also set the volume by using the volume slider on the play control bar.
2. Under **Video Tools - Playback** tab, in the **Video Options** group, *click* **Volume**, and then choose one of the following:

- Low
- Medium
- High
- Mute

Loop a video

To play your video repeatedly and continuously during your presentation, you can use the loop feature.

1. Select the video that you would like to loop.

2. Under **Video Tools - Playback** tab, in the **Video Options** group, select the **Loop until Stopped** check box.

Rewind a video after playing

To rewind your video after playing during your presentation, do the following:

1. Select the video that you would like to rewind.
2. Under **Video Tools - Playback** tab, in the **Video Options** group, select the **Rewind after Playing** check box.

Show the media controls

To show the media controls during your presentation, do the following:

1. Select the video that you would like to show the medial controls on.
2. On the **Slide Show** tab, in the **Set up** group, select the **Show Media Controls** check box.

Start or end your video with a fade effect

You can start or end your video with a fade effect for a specified number of seconds.

1. Select the video on the slide.
2. Under **Video Tools - Playback** tab, in the **Editing** group, under **Fade Duration**, do one or both of the following:

- To add a timed fade to the beginning of your video, in the **Fade In** box, *click* the up and down arrows to increase or decrease the **Fade In** time.
- To add a timed fade to the end of your video, in the **Fade Out** box, *click* the up or down arrows to increase or decrease the **Fade Out** time.

Text Overlay with Videos

You can add and synchronize descriptive overlay text to fade in and out while your video plays.

Add text as an overlay to your video

You may want to overlay the video with a note or some company information. To do so you can add text on top of the video. This does not serve any real purpose except if you forgot to watermark the video and as a second though you wanted to include company logo or some copyright information above the video.

1. Display the slide on which you've inserted the video. Do not select the video.
2. On the **Insert** tab, in the **Text** group, *click* **Text Box**. You may have to select **Horizontal** or **Vertical Text Box**.
3. Point to the area on the video where you want the text to appear, and then *drag* to draw the text box.
4. Enter the text in the text box. You may need to manually change the color of your text so that it stands out from the background of the video as it plays. If you play the video full screen the text will not appear on the video, only when the video is

played at the size you selected on the slide will you see the text overlay.

Video Poster Frame

A poster frame is the frame that shows before the video is played. If no poster frame is selected most likely a black frame will be on the slide, or the first frame of the video.

1. *Click* **Video Tools – Playback** tab.
2. *Click* **Play** to begin playing the video.
3. Play the video until you see the frame that you want to use as your poster frame, and then *click* **Pause**.
4. *Click* **Video Tools - Format** tab.
5. In the **Adjust** group, *click* **Poster Frame**.
6. *Click* **Current Frame.**

Use a picture as a poster frame

1. Select the video on the slide.
2. *Click* **Video Tools - Format** tab.
3. In the **Adjust** group, *click* **Poster Frame,** and then *click* **Image from file**.
4. The **Insert Picture** dialog window appears. Select the picture you would like.
5. *Click* **Insert**

Video Brightness and Contrast

You can adjust the brightness of a video (relative lightness) and the difference between the darkest and lightest areas of a video (contrast).

Change the brightness of a video

1. Select the video on the slide.
2. *Click* **Video Tools -Format** tab.
3. In the **Adjust** group, *click* **Correction**.
4. *Click* the **Brightness and Contrast** setting that you want. By moving your mouse pointer over the examples of effects a live preview feature in PowerPoint lets you see what your video will look like prior to *clicking* on your choice.

You can get more options and more control over the brightness and contrast by *clicking* on **Video Correction Options** at the bottom of the dialog window.

1. When the **Format Video** dialog window opens *click* on **Video**.
2. The Format Video dialog window has two sections: **Recolor** and **Brightness and Contrast** where further alterations can be set.
3. You can also **Reset** the brightness and contrast to the original settings by *clicking* on the **Reset** button.

Borders around Videos

You can add a border to your video and then change the color of the border. You can also change the look of the line style or the weight of the line. This can give your video a more professional look and give the appearance of watching a movie or television.

Change the color of a border

1. Select the video on the slide.
2. *Click* the **Video Tools - Format** tab.
3. In the **Video Styles** group, *click* the arrow next to **Video Border.**
4. *Click* the color that you want.
5. If you don't see the **Video Tools - Format** tabs, make sure that you've selected the video.
6. To change to a color that is not in the theme colors, *click* **More Outline Colors**, and then either *click* the color that you want on the **Standard** tab, or mix your own color on the **Custom** tab.

Change the style of a border

1. Select the video on the slide.
2. Under **Video Tools - Format** tab, in the **Video Styles** group, *click* the arrow next to **Video Border**. If you don't see the **Video Tools - Format** tabs, make sure that you've selected the video.
3. Move your mouse over **Dashes**, and then select the line style that you want.

a. To create a custom style, *click* **More Lines**, the **Format Video** dialog window will open. Here you can choose the options that you want.

Change the weight of a border

1. Select the video on the slide.
2. Under **Video Tools - Format** tab, in the **Video Styles** group, *click* the arrow next to **Video Border**. If you don't see the **Video Tools** - **Format** tabs, make sure that you've selected the video.
3. Move your mouse over **Weight**, and then select the line weight that you want.
   a. To create a custom style, *click* **More Lines**, the **Format Video** dialog window will open. Here you can choose the options that you want.

Delete a border

1. Select the shape that you want to change.
2. Under **Video Tools - Format** tab, in the **Video Styles** group, *click* the arrow next to **Video Border**. If you don't see the **Video Tools** - **Format** tabs, make sure that you've selected the video.
3. *Click* on **No Outline**.

Deleting a Video

1. Click on the video or animated GIF.
2. Push the **Delete** key on your computer's keypad.
3. Or *right-click* your mouse and select **Cut**.
4. If your video or animated GIF does not delete, the media has been inserted in the slide master or associated layout.
5. To delete a video or animated GIF file from a slide master, on the **View** tab, in the **Master Views** group, click **Slide Master**. In **Master View**, select the slide master or layout that contains the unwanted media. Push the **Delete** key on the keypad.

Optimize Compatibility

If you are having trouble playing or inserting media, it could be that PowerPoint cannot work with the file extension type. The best solution is to run **Optimize Compatibility**. Or try downloading a third-party media decoder and encoder filter, which will allow you to decode and encode a variety of formats.

When using both the Apple's Office for Mac and the PC's and running your presentation on both, you could have media compatibility problems. If you decide to deliver the presentation that you created on a PC, on an Apple Macintosh, the file format WMV and WMA are not native to a Macintosh computer. In this case you will need an Internet connection so that you can download a QuickTime component (for the Mac operating system) that supports Windows Media Video, such as Flip4Mac, to play these your media files.

The **Optimize Compatibility** command in PowerPoint will help you to resolve playback issues. To avoid playback issues when your PowerPoint presentation contains media, such as animated GIF files, video files or audio files, you can optimize the media files for compatibility. This makes it easy to share your presentation with others or so you can take the presentation to another computer at the location that you will be giving the presentation, and be sure that your slideshow will play correctly.

1. When you are ready to share your presentation, with the presentation open in PowerPoint, on the **File** tab, *click* **Info**.
2. *Click* on **Optimize Compatibility** button.
3. The **Optimize Media Compatibility** window will open and run the compatibility test.
4. When the test is complete the Status will state that it is **Complete**. *Click* the **Close** button.

When the **Optimize Compatibility** appears, it provides a summarization for resolutions of potential playback issues. It also provides a list of the number of occurrences of media in the presentation. The following are common scenarios that can cause playback issues:

1. If you have linked videos, the **Optimize Media Compatibility** summarization will report that you need to embed them. *Click* the **View Links** option to proceed. The dialog box that opens will allow you to embed the videos simply by *clicking* **Break Link** for each media item that you want to embed.
2. If you have videos that were inserted using an earlier version of PowerPoint, such as version 2007,

you will need to upgrade your media file format in order to ensure that these files will play back. Upgrading will automatically update and embed these media items to the new format. Once you have upgraded, you should run the **Optimize for Compatibility** command.

Converting Older Videos

To upgrade your media files from an earlier version to PowerPoint 2010, on the **File** tab, *click* **Info**, and then *click* **Manage Versions**. Note that the Manage Versions button will not be an option if the presentation was developed in PowerPoint 2010.

Making Videos from Presentations

You can now save your Microsoft PowerPoint 2010 presentation as a video, making it easier for you to distribute, and easier for recipients to view.

In PowerPoint 2010, you can now save your presentation as a Windows Media Video (WMV) file, and distribute it knowing that your animated, narrated, multimedia presentation will play without a glitch. If you do not want to use the WMV file format, you can use a preferred third party utility to convert your file to another format (.avi, .mov, etc).

Some tips to remember when recording your presentation as a video:

- You can record voice narration in your video.
- You can record laser pointer movements in your video.

- You can control the size of the multimedia file and the quality of your video.
- You can include animations and transitions in your movie.
- Viewers do not need to have PowerPoint installed on their computers to watch it.
- If your presentation contains an embedded video, the video will play correctly without your needing to control it.

Depending on the content of your presentation, creating a video may take some time. Lengthy presentations and presentations with animations, transitions, and media content will likely take longer to create.

Record and Time Voice Narration and Pointer Movements

To record and playback a narration, your computer must be equipped with a sound card, microphone, and speakers. Some third-party software will also let you have picture-in-picture (PIP), in this case you will need a webcam.

If you are going to distribute the video to customers or to YouTube, it is a good idea to include music or audio that either reinforce your message or makes your video entertaining. Audio quality is very important when making a video. A good microphone and no background noise is preferred if you want to come across as a professional. When creating a video version of a presentation, you'll probably want to "capture" the human element of the presentation by recording and timing voice narration and even laser pointer gestures. PowerPoint will also let you write on the presentation when recording.

You can record your audio prior to recording the slide show and then combine the slide show and the audio at the time of recording. If you use a webcam or a video camera you can record a narration while actively delivering a presentation to a live audience while capturing both the slide show and the video.

Recording Slide Shows

If you want to make your slide show into a video you first need to record your slide show. There are several things you need to do first to make sure that the presentations; audio, transitions, animations and narratives are captured.

Under Slide Show tab make sure that the following are checked.

1. Play Narrations
2. Use Timings
3. Show Media Controls

Recording the Slide Show

1. Make sure that your microphone is plugged in and properly working.
2. *Click* on **Slide Show** tab.
3. *Click* on **Record Slide Show** drop down arrow under the **Set Up** group.
4. *Click* on **Start Recording from Beginning**. The **Record Slide Show** dialog window opens.
5. Make sure both **Slide and Animation Timings and Narrations** and **Laser Pointer** boxes are checked.
6. *Click* **Start Recording**.
7. Move through your presentation and talk into the microphone.

8. When done, it can take a long time before the recorded slide show will finish and return to PowerPoint **Slide Sorter** screen.
9. In the **Slide Sorter** screen you will notice that each slide will have a time in the lower left corner. This is the timing for each slide. The default time spent on each slide is set to 5 seconds. To change that to the right of seconds to spend on each slide, *click* the up arrow to increase, or the down arrow to decrease the seconds.

Save as a Video

Once you have created your presentation follow these steps to make your presentation into a video.

1. On the **File** menu, *click* **Save & Send.**
2. Under **Save & Send**, *click* **Create a video.**
3. To display all video quality and size options, under **Create a video**, *click* the **Computer & HD Displays** down arrow.
4. Do one of the following:

- To create a video with very high quality, yet a large file size, *click* **Computer & HD Displays.**
- To create a video with a moderate file size and medium quality, *click* **Internet & DVD.**
- To create a video with the smallest file size, yet low quality, *click* **Portable Devices.**

5. *Click* the **Don't Use Recorded Timings and Narrations** down arrow and then, do one of the following:

- If you did not record and time voice narration and laser pointer movements, *click* **Don't Use Recorded Timings and Narration**.
- If you recorded and timed narration and pointer movements, *click* **Use Recorded Timings and Narrations.**

6. *Click* **Create Video.**
7. In the **File name** box, enter a file name for the video, browse for folder that will contain this file, and then *click* **Save**. You can track the progress of the video creation by looking at the status bar at the bottom of your screen. The video creation process can take up to several hours depending on the length of the video and the complexity of the presentation.
8. To play your newly created video, go to the designated folder location, and then *double-click* the file. Most of the time the video can be found in the My Video file.

Making a Video

If you have old PowerPoint presentations that you want to use, it is easy to convert these into video. As a matter of fact, there are many ways to turn PowerPoint presentations into videos. Once these presentations are in a movie format they are easy to add to most video editing software, where the video editor can add sound, voice, text, movement and animation. Most likely if you have PowerPoint presentations you're a Windows user. Therefore it is easy to use the Windows free applications to change your PowerPoint presentation into photo format or perform a screen capture to make a video.

Screen Capture (Screen casting)

The first method that I would like to show you is performing a screen capture of your presentation, and then editing it on video editing software. First you need to change the PowerPoint presentation to a slide show. The best way to do this is to go into the slide show's rehearsed timing.

1. Go to **Slide Show** in the toolbar and *click* on **Rehearse Timings**.
2. Go through the slide show as if you were giving a presentation, moving through the slide show by *clicking* the screen at the time intervals that you would like. Go through each slide and review what you would like to say. You do not have to have any sound or voice-over at this time, as you can add this through the video editing software.
3. As you go through the rehearsed timing, make sure that you give yourself enough time on each slide. It's OK if the slide timing is too long, because you'll be able to adjust the time on the video editing

software. In fact, it is better to have extra time on each slide than to be short. Although all your video editing software can let you freeze or slow the frame speed, it is better and easier to shorten a frame than try to extend the length.

4. After going through the rehearsed timing, you will want to review your slide show and make sure that you have enough time to say what is needed. Make any changes at this time.
5. Next you need to save your PowerPoint slide show as a **PPS** file (for Office 2003) or a **PPSX** file (for Office 2007 or later).
6. To save the PowerPoint presentation to a slide show ppsx file, follow these steps.
    a. *Click* on **File**.
    b. *Click* on **Save As**.
    c. Give the presentation a name.
    d. Under **Save as Type**: select **PowerPoint Show.**
    e. *Click* **Save**.
7. Next, make sure that you have downloaded Windows Media Encoder, or a screencast (screen-captured) third party's software. You can download Windows Media Encoder from www.Microsoft.com or typing "Windows Media Encoder" in your search engine. This is free software from Microsoft to perform the screen capture. You may have to do a search for Windows Media Encoder© on the

Microsoft web page. With Windows Media Encoder you can either do a screen capture video or capture video from a webcam. There are many third party screen capture programs. Many are more powerful than Windows Media Encoder and they have many features that Windows Media Encoder doesn't have.

8. Open up the screen capture software.
9. Capture the presentation.

Every screen capture or screen casting software will have their own set of instructions. Below you will find examples of two, Windows Media Encoder and Camtasia (a very popular third party software).

Windows Media Encoder

For the Microsoft Media Encoder do the following: (Note: Different series of Windows Media Encoder may have different instructions.)

1. To capture the screen video, go in to Windows Media Encoder, *click* on Capture Screen; make sure you *click* on the box for the entire screen. If you would like to add audio at this time make sure that you *click* the box that lets you capture audio from a default audio device, otherwise make sure that this box is unchecked.
2. Next, put in the name and location where you would like to save the new file, then *click* **Next**.
3. Make sure that you *click* the boxes for **high-quality** then *click* **Next**.

4. The next page is **Display Information**, put in your Title, Author, copyright information and a description of what the video is about. *Click* **Next**.
5. The next page is just a verification of the information that you put in, if it is incorrect go back and change the information. Make sure you *click* the box that says "**Begin Capturing Screens When I Click Finish**". Then *click* **OK**.
6. *Click* on the PowerPoint presentation and make sure that you move the mouse cursor off the screen so it is no longer visible; otherwise it will show up in your video. When the PowerPoint presentation is over, push ***ESC*** on your keyboard to go back to the Windows Media Encoder, and stop the recording.

You have now made a WMV file. This file can be played on Real Player or Windows Media Player. If you use Windows Movie Maker as your video editing software, you can load/insert this video into the editing software and you are ready to begin editing and adding the sound and animations you want.

You can also use Windows Media Encoder to capture video with your webcam. Instead of going into **Capture Screen** as we did in the previous example, you would go into **Capture Audio and Video**. The main difference is that you have to fill out the **Device Options** page. The information on this page specifies what device you are using to capture the video and audio. The rest of the procedures are the same as for the **Capture Screen** instructions given above.

Camtasia

I have included Camtasia in this book for several reasons. First it is a very popular screen cast or screen capture software. Second reason I included it is because it is easy to use and is an Add-in for PowerPoint. And the third reason I included Camtasia in this book is because it is what I use. As I mentioned Camtasia is an Add-in for PowerPoint, which means that it is available in the ribbon under the Add-Ins tab.

With Camtasia you do not have to record timing and narration before recording, this is done while in Camtasia.

The commands for Camtasia are:

- Record
- Record Audio - Records from your microphone or the built-in default microphone. For best quality use an USB microphone.
- Record Camera – This is for your webcam to record what you are doing during the presentation.
- Show Camera Preview – Lets you preview what the camera will record.
- Recording Options – Opens up an Options dialog window for further detail adjustments.
- Help

Before you start recording it is best to turn off the timing and narrations that might have been recorded previously.

When ready just *click* on the **Record** button and you will have a dialog box open that will let you test the sound.

Click the **red record button** and the recording will count down for you to begin recording. When done push the ***Esc*** key and a Camtasia dialog window will open. You can stop the recording or continue. When you stop the recording a **Save Camtasia Recording** dialog window will open. Give the file and name and *click* **Save**. Another Camtasia Studio dialog window will open with two options:

- Produce Your Recording
- Edit Your Recording

Select **Edit Your Recording** to open Camtasia for video editing.

After the recording Camtasia will open and you can make professional video editing changes and have special tools that will let you add captions, titles, music and much more. You can zoom in and out of special areas of the presentation and add mouse highlights and other special effects.

Saving PowerPoint slides as Pictures

The second way to make a video from your PowerPoint presentations is to save the PowerPoint presentation as pictures by using the **Save** command, and saving the presentation as either a JPEG or a PNG file. This will save each slide as a picture (or still image), which can be loaded directly into the video editing software. With this method you will lose all animations, transitions and sound that you had with the presentation. You can make several slides from one slide to give the video the animation effect of adding text, bullets, and images as the video progresses.

1. *Click* on **File** tab.
2. *Click* on **Save & Send**.

3. Under **File Types**, *click* on **Change File Type**.
4. Under **Image File Types** *click* one of the following:

- PNG Portable Network Graphics
- JPEG File Interchange Format

5. *Click* **Save As** button.
6. The **Save As** dialog window opens. Give your presentation a name. *Click* **Save**.
7. Microsoft PowerPoint dialog box opens asking "Do you want to export every slide in the presentation or only the current slide". *Click* one of the following buttons:

- Every Slide
- Current Slide Only
- Cancel.

8. If you selected **Every Slide**, you now have a folder with every slide as a picture.
9. Transfer the pictures to a movie editing software and make the edits to the pictures and add voice and music.

Using PowerPoint File to make a video

PowerPoint 2010 as a new feature that lets you uses the PowerPoint presentations into a video without a lot of headaches. You can use the recording timings and the narratives or you can use the recording timing defaults in PowerPoint.

1. *Click* on **File**.
2. *Click* on **Save & Send**.
3. Under **File Types**, *click* on **Create a Video**.

4. Under the first dropdown box you have three options:

- Computer & HD Displays.
- Internet & DVD
- Portable Devises

5. Under the second dropdown box you have three options:

- Use Recorded Timings and Narrations.
- Don't Use Recorded Timings and Narrations.
- You can also Record Timings and Narrations or Review Timings and Narrations under this dropdown option.

6. Make a choice and *click* **Create Video**.
7. The **Window Save As** dialog window opens. Give your video a name, and *click* **Save**. The process may take some time before your presentation is converted to a video format.

You now have the file in WMV format. If you use Windows Movie Maker, Sony Vegas, or Adobe Premiere, you can load the WMV file into the editing software and start making a professional video. If you use Apple's Final Cut Pro, you need to convert the WMV file to an AVI file format. Simply download or insert this video file on a separate track in any one of the video editing software products and you can edit this software just like you would any other video.

What to do with your video after creating it?

After you create a video, you can share it with others by using the following methods:

- Use e-mail to send a presentation or a link to a presentation
- Burn your slide show to a DVD disc
- Upload it to a video sharing Web site, such as YouTube
- Save to a file share or other location

Uploading to Social Media Sites

If you want to share your presentation with the world you can make your presentation a video and allow others to view and share your presentation on the Web. Social media sites like YouTube are a great way to distribute information and keep track of who is viewing your presentation. Publishing your slide show video to YouTube is one of the easiest ways to host it online free of charge and take advantage of the World Wide Web exposure. There are many other social media sites that will host your video for free. Here are some simple steps to give you the general idea of the process that you need to complete to get your video on the web.

- In PowerPoint 2010, create a video from your slide show.
- You can use the free download Windows Movie Maker, Windows Live or a third party screen capture-edit software.
- You will have to have a YouTube account (or an account in the social media web site that you are trying to publish to.
- Most of the social media sites except a wide variety of file types and then convert your file format to a

Flash format (SWF), so you do not have to worry about the file format.

- Most third party software will have buttons to publish your video. Look for commands like **Sharing** or **Publish.** Some will have special buttons for **Publishing on YouTube**. You can also go to the Social Media site and upload your video from their site.
- Some third party software will Add-In to PowerPoint and you will be able to capture the screen, the audio, and use your webcam to capture yourself presenting the PowerPoint presentation.

Publish to Windows Live©

Microsoft PowerPoint 2010 enables you to save your presentation to Web sites such as Windows Live for others to access. You can save a presentation to the Web as a PowerPoint (.pptx or .ppt) file, a PDF or other file type.

PowerPoint 2010 does not support saving a PowerPoint file as a Web page. These are the instructions for Windows Live.

1. Open the presentation that you want to publish to the Web.
2. *Click* the **File** tab, and then *click* **Save & Send**.
3. Under **Save & Send**, *click* **Save to Web**.
    a. If you want people to have access to a presentation that you published to the Web, you must specify a Web server or other available computer when you choose a

location for the file. Some Web sites, such as Windows Live, may require you to sign in to connect to the server on which your presentation is to be saved.

4. *Click* **Sign In.** This will bring up a **Sign In** dialog box.

☑ Tips for improving audio and video playback and compatibility

If you experience slow playback, a lag between audio and video, audio stuttering, and frames being lost, the following steps can help to help improve the audio and video playback and compatibility of your media-based presentation.

Improve playback performance

- Make your PowerPoint presentation smaller and improve playback performance by compressing your media files.
- Install more memory or a more powerful graphics card on the computer.
- Limit or remove special effects in your media, such as shadows, reflections, glow effects, soft edges, bevels, and 3-D rotation to a video, from your video.
- Optimize the media in your presentation for compatibility to guarantee the best possible playback performance.

- Or you can use a third-party vendor's software to record the PowerPoint presentation into a video. Third-party software also can give you the option of picture-in-picture recording with your webcam.

Considerations for linking or embedding

When your presentation contains video or audio files it is a good idea to embed them instead of linking them. Embedding media files will guarantee their playback, but will also make the presentation file significantly larger. Linking files will allow you to change or update the media file. However, it is not possible to optimize linked video or audio files for compatibility. If the media is embedded, you'll want to optimize the media in your presentation for compatibility.

If you must link to videos instead of embedding them, make sure that you have a working network connection at the site where you plan to deliver your presentation, plus put all the linked files in the same folder. Also, be sure to test the connection before presenting. This will help you to identify problems before you start the presentation. A benefit of linking to the media is that the presentation file size will be smaller. However, be sure to copy the linked media files into the same directory file as the presentation so that they will surely play.

You can also compress your presentation so that no space is wasted. Follow these steps to compress the file:

1. *Click* on **File** tab.
2. *Click* **Info**,
3. *Click* **Compress Media**, you will have three choices:

- Presentation Quality – Highest quality.
- Internet Quality – Middle quality.
- Low Quality – As the name indicates, low quality.

4. Low Quality would compress the file the most. Remember you will lose some of the quality and this may be noticeable when viewing.

Chapter 19 Sharing the Presentation

As with any software program, it is a good idea to name and save your presentation immediately and then to save your changes frequently while you work:

1. *Click* the **File** tab.
2. *Click* **Save As**, and then do one of the following:
3. For a presentation that can be opened only in PowerPoint 2010 or PowerPoint 2007, in the **Save as type** list, select **PowerPoint Presentation (*.PPTX)**.
4. For a presentation that can be opened in either PowerPoint 2003 or earlier versions of PowerPoint, select **PowerPoint 97-2003 Presentation (*.PPT)**.
5. On the left-hand pane in the **Save As** dialog box, *click* the folder or other location where you want to save your presentation.
6. In the **File name** box, type a name for your presentation, or do nothing to accept the default file name, and then *click* **Save**.

Key boards shortcut for saving is *CTRL+S*, you can also *click* the **Save icon** in the **Quick Access Toolbar.**

Changing Page Size

If you change the slide size or orientation after you add content, the content may be rescaled. You could have to go back and readjust every page. So it will save you time to set up the page size prior to adding content. To set up your presentation prior to adding content do the following steps.

1. *Click* on the **Design** tab.
2. In the **Page Setup** group, *click* **Page Setup**.
3. In the **Slides sized for** list, *click* the size of paper on which you will be printing or select the view size that you would like for a video.

- If you *click* **Custom**, you will have to type or select the measurements that you want in the **Width** and **Height** boxes.
- To print an overhead transparency, *click* **Overhead**.
- If you are making a wide screen video *chick* **On-Screen Show (16:9)**

4. To set the slide's orientation, under **Orientation**, under **Slides**, *click* **Landscape** or **Portrait**. By default, PowerPoint slide layouts appear in landscape orientation.
5. In the **Number slides from** box, enter the number that you want to print on the first slide or page one of the handouts, with subsequent slides or pages numbered after it.

Setting Print Options

To set your printing options (including number of copies, printer, slides to print, number of slides per page, color options, and more) and then print your slides, do the following:

1. *Click* the **File** tab.
2. *Click* **Print**, and then under **Print**, in the **Copies** box, enter the number of copies that you want to print.

3. Under **Printer**, select the printer that you want to use.
4. Under **Settings**, *click* on **Print Selection** and do one of the following:

- To print all slides, *click* **Print All Slides**.
- To print one or more slides that you selected, *click* **Print Selection**.
- To select multiple slides to print, *click* the **Home** tab, and then in **Normal** view, in the left-hand pane that contains the **Outline and Slides** tabs, *click* the **Slides** tab and then *press and hold CTRL* while you select the slides that you want. Then go back to **File – Print** and *click* **Print Selection** and *click* **Print Selection.**
- To print only the slide that is currently displayed, *click* **Print Current Slide.**
- To print specific slides by number, *click* **Custom Range**, and then enter a list of individual slides, a range, or both. Use commas to separate the numbers and no spaces, for example, 1,3,5-12.

5. Under **Settings** you can also *click* on **Full Page Slides** and have options for **Print Layout** or **Handouts**:
   a. Print Layout
   b. Full Page Slides
   c. Notes Pages
   d. Outlines
   e. Handouts

f. Number of slides per page and printed Horizontal or Vertical.

To print a thin border around your slides, select **Frame Slides**. This is a check / uncheck option. *Click* it again to deselect it and prevent a border from printing.

To print your slides on the paper that you selected for your printer, *click* **Scale to Fit Paper**.

To increase resolution, blend transparent graphics, and print soft shadows in your print job, *click* **High quality**. This may take longer for your presentation to print.

1. To print on both sides of your handouts *click* **Print One Sided** and the select **Print On Both Sides**.
2. *Click* **Collated**, and then choose whether you want your slides to print **Collated** or **Uncollated**.
3. *Click* **Color**, and then *click* one of the following:

- **Color**. This option prints in color to a color printer. Remove color backgrounds from your presentation. On the **Design** tab, in the **Background** group, *click* **Background Styles**, and then *click* the upper left example. This is a plain white background.
- **Grayscale.** This option prints images that contain variations of gray tones between black and white. Background fills are printed as white, so that the text will be more legible. (Sometimes grayscale appears the same as **Pure Black and White**.)
- **Pure Black and White.** This option prints the handout without gray fills.

4. To include or change headers and footers, *click* the **Edit Header and Footer** link, and then make your selections in the **Header and Footer** dialog box that appears.
5. *Click* **Print** at the top of the screen.

Save Print Settings

If you want to reset the print options and keep them as your default settings, do the following:

1 *Click* the **File** tab.

2 Under **Help**, *click* **Options**, and then *click* **Advanced**.

3 Under **When printing this document**, *click* the **Option Box** next to **Use The Most Recently Used Print Settings**, and then *click* **OK**.

Printing and Print Review

On the **File - Print** tab, the properties for your default printer automatically appear in the left section, and the preview of your presentation automatically appears in the right section.

1 *Click* the **File** tab, and then *click* **Print**.

2 You can view what slides will be printed by scrolling down the presentation on the right side of the screen.

3 When the properties for your printer and presentation appear the way that you want them to, *click* **Print**.

Edit or Print Handouts in Word

You can print handouts from Microsoft PowerPoint 2010, but if you want to use the editing and formatting features of Microsoft Word, you can work on and print your handouts using Word. In the open presentation, do the following:

1 *Click* the **File** tab and then *click* **Save & Send**.

2 Under **File Types**, *click* **Create Handouts**, and then under **Create Handouts in Microsoft Word**, *click* **Create Handouts**.

3 In the **Send to Microsoft Office Word** dialog box, *click* the page layout that you want, and then do one of the following:

- To paste content that you want to remain unchanged when the content in the original PowerPoint presentation is updated, *click* **Paste**, and then *click* **OK**.
- To ensure that any updates that occur to the original PowerPoint presentation are reflected in the Word document, *click* **Paste Link**, and then *click* **OK**.
- The presentation opens as a Word document in a new window. This can take some time to open every slide. You can edit, print or save as with any Word document.

Self-Running Presentation

By using a self-running presentation created in Microsoft PowerPoint 2010, you can communicate your information without a presenter. For example, you can set up a presentation to run unattended in a booth or kiosk at a trade show or convention, or you can send a CD with a self-running presentation to a client.

You can make most controls unavailable, so that your audience cannot make changes to your self-running presentation. Self-running presentations restart after they are finished and when they have been idle on a manually advanced slide for longer than five minutes.

Set up a Self-Running Presentation

To set up a PowerPoint presentation to run automatically, do the following:

1 On the **Slide Show** tab, in the **Set Up** group, *click* **Set Up Slide Show**.

2 In the **Set Up Show** box, under **Show type**, do one of the following:

- *Click* **Browsed By an Individual (Window)** *Click* this if you do not want the individual to have to *click* to advance to the next slide.
- *Click* **Browsed at a Kiosk (Full Screen)**.

3 Under the **Show Options** section check the box for **Loop Continuously Until 'Esc'.**

4 If you have used audio, make sure to uncheck the box for **Show Without Narration.**

5 If you do not want to show the animation, and you just want the slides to advance to the next slide, check the box **Show Without Animation.**

If you use **Presented by a Speaker (Full Screen)** make sure that you uncheck the **Use Timings** check box in the **Set Up** group under the **Slide Show** tab. Otherwise the presentation will run automatically and the speaker (presenter) will not have control over the timing of the slides. The main thing to remember for a self-running presentation is to set timing and make sure that the **Use Timing** check box in the **Set Up** group is check.

If you set up a self-running presentation, remember to set slide timing options by *clicking* on the **Rehearse Timings** tab in the **Set Up** group. A self-running presentation will have problems with navigation hyperlinks to other documents or Internet sites, or action buttons such as graphics. You can set up the slide show to let users *click* to go forward or back in the presentation. Otherwise, your self-running presentation will not advance beyond the first slide.

Rehearse and Record Slide Timings

If you want a self-running slide show or you want to show the slide show as a video, setting the time is important. If you are using audio (Narrations) and using screen-capture software the timing is not as important. When recording for video you will want to advance the slides as you record the audio. See more about this in the video section of this book. Once you set the slide to run as a self-running slide show, you need to set the timing.

1 Make sure that the **Use Timing** check box in the **Set Up** group under the **Slide Show** tab is checked.

2 On the **Slide Show** tab, in the **Set Up** group, *click* **Rehearse Timings**.

3 The **Rehearsal** toolbar appears and the **Slide Time** box begins timing the presentation.

4 You can advance to the next animated object or the next page by doing one of the following:

- *Click* on the arrow in the Recording dialog window.
- *Click* your mouse button.
- Hit the space bar.
- Hit the right arrow or down arrow keys on the keyboard.

5 Push to '***Esc'*** key to exit the slide show. A window will appear telling you the total slide show time, and ask if you would like to keep the time.

The **Rehearsal toolbar (Recording)** is in the upper left hand corner. It will not be visible on the slide show or video if you are recording the screen. The **Rehearsal** toolbar consist of the following sections.

- **Next** (advance to next slide). This can be used instead of *clicking* the left mouse button or the space bar.
- **Pause**. If you need to pause the timing, use this button. A Resume Recording window will appear in the middle of the slide show. *Click* the Resume Recording button to continue.
- **Slide Time**. This is the time recorded for the present slide.
- **Repeat**. If you want to start over on the present slide use this button. It will start the slide time back at 0:00:00.
- **Total presentation time**. This is the time that has been recorded for the slide show up to the slide you are on. At the end of the recording this will be the total time recorded.

After you set the time for the last slide, a message box displays the total time for the presentation and prompts you to do one of the following:

- To keep the recorded slide timings, *click* **Yes**. **Slide Sorter** view appears and displays the time of each slide in your presentation.
- To discard the recorded slide timings, *click* **No**.

Add narration

Adding narration can help deliver information more clearly in your self-running presentation. You will want to use narration also when you are using screen capture software to record a video. Or you can record narration in a third-party video editing software.

To record a narration, your computer requires a sound card and a microphone. You can record a narration before you run a presentation, or you can record it during the presentation and include audience comments. If you do not want narration throughout your entire presentation, you can record separate sounds or comments on selected slides or objects.

Set the slide timings manually

PowerPoint 2010 will automatically record your slide timings when you add narration or you can manually set the slide timings to accompany your narrations.

1 In **Normal** view, *click* the slide that you want to set the timing for.

2 On the **Transitions** tab, in the **Timing** group, under **Advance Slide**, select the **After** check box, and then enter the number of seconds that you want the

slide to appear on the screen. Repeat the process for each slide that you want to set the timing for.

If you want the next slide to appear either when you *click* the mouse or automatically after the number of seconds that you enter — whichever comes first — select both the **On Mouse Click** and the **After** check boxes. (Under the **Transitions** tab).

Turn the slide timings off

Turning off the slide timings does not delete them. You can turn the timings back on at any time without having to recreate them. However, when the slide timings are turned off, your slides will not automatically advance when you record a narration, and you will need to manually advance the slides.

1 In Normal view, on the **Slide Show** tab, in the **Set Up** group, *click* **Set Up Slide Show.**

2 Under **Advance slides**, *click* **Manually**.

3 To turn the timings back on, under **Advance slides**, *click* **Using Timings, If Present.**

This also can be done in one step by un-checking the **Use Timings** box in the **Set up** group under the **Slide Show** tab.

Chapter 20 Packaging for CD

Burning Slide Shows to a CD

Anyone with a standard DVD or disc player can watch and enjoy a PowerPoint presentation or photo album that you create. You'll need both a DVD or disc burner and Windows DVD Maker (or another 3rd party DVD burning software).

1. Create a slide show using timing to make the slide show self-running.
2. *Click* on **File**
3. *Click* on **Save As**. The **Save As** dialog window opens.
4. Give the file a name.
5. In the **Save as Type** drop down list, choose **PowerPoint Show.**
6. *Click* **Save**
7. *Click* on **File**.
8. *Click* on **Save & Send.**
9. *Click* on **Package Presentation for CD**. This will assure that the linked items will be included in the presentation. For example, if you used an Excel worksheet for a chart, the Package Presentation for CD will put the worksheet with the PowerPoint to make the presentation work as you planned.
10. *Click* **Package for CD**.
11. The Package for CD dialog window opens. Name the CD. Under the files to be copied, if you saved

the presentation as PowerPoint Show, you should have a PPSX file type.

12. If you want to add other files to the CD, *click* the **Add** button.
13. *Click* **Copy to CD**.
14. There may be a Warning window that pops up on your screen, warning you to include all the linked files to your presentation. *Click* **Yes**. The presentation will copy to the CD. Make sure that you put a CD in your CD burner drive.
15. When you want to view the presentation you may have to download Microsoft Presentation Viewer software.

Chapter 21 Improving the Presentation

Create a Slide Layout

If you do not find a standard layout that meets your needs, you can customize an existing layout that perfectly suits your slide content.

1 On the **View** tab, in the **Master Views** group, *click* **Slide Master**.

2 In the pane that contains the slide masters and layouts, locate and *click* the layout that resembles the closest match to what you want in your custom layout.

Types of Layouts:

1. Firelight Slide master
2. Title Slide Layout
3. Title and Content Layout
4. Section Header Layout
5. Two Content Layout
6. Comparison Layout
7. Title Only Layout
8. Blank Layout
9. Content with Caption Layout
10. Picture with Caption Layout
11. Title and Vertical Text Layout
12. Vertical Title and Text Layout

If none of the layouts meet your needs, select the **Blank Layout**, or modify one of the layouts. To modify the layout, do one or more of the following:

1. To remove unwanted, default placeholders such as headers, footers, or the date and time, *click* the border of the placeholder, and then press **Delete**.
2. To add a placeholder, do the following:
    a. On the **Slide Master** tab, in the **Master Layout** group, *click* **Insert Placeholder**, and then select a placeholder type from the list.
    b. *Click* a location on the layout, and then *drag* to draw the placeholder.
    c. To resize a placeholder, select one of the sizing handles or corner borders, *click and drag* the corner in or out.
3. To rename the layout: In the thumbnail list of layouts, *right-click* the layout that you customized, and then *click* **Rename Layout**.
4. In the **Rename Layout** dialog box, type a new name that describes the layout you've just created, and then *click* **Rename**.
5. To save the custom layout in a template, on the **File** tab, under **Saving**, *click* **Save As**.
6. In the **File name** box, type a file name, or accept the suggested file name.
7. In the **Save as type** list, *click* **PowerPoint Template**, and then *click* **Save**.
8. Close **Master** view by *clicking* **Normal** under the **View** tab.

9. The layout that you added and customized now appears in the list of standard, built-in layouts in **Normal** view, located on the **Home** tab, in the **Slides** group, under the **Layout** drop down list.

Portrait & Landscape Orientation

By default, Microsoft PowerPoint 2010 slide layouts are set up in landscape orientation the other choice is Portrait page orientation. To change all the slides in your presentation to portrait orientation do the following:

1. *Click* on the **Design** tab.
2. In the **Page Setup** group, *click* **Slide Orientation**
3. *Click* **Portrait**.

A presentation can have only one orientation (either landscape or portrait), but you can link two presentations (one in landscape, and the other in portrait) to display both portrait and landscape slides in what appears to be one presentation. To link two presentations, do the following:

Place both presentations in the same folder before you create links. That way, if the folder is copied to a CD or moved, the presentations will still link correctly.

1. Create a link from the first presentation to the second presentation:
    a. In the first presentation, select the text or object that you want to *click* to link to the second presentation.
    b. On the **Insert** tab, in the **Links** group, *click* **Action**.

c. In the **Action Settings** dialog box, on either the **Mouse Click** tab or **Mouse Over** tab, *click* **Hyperlink To**, and then *click* **Other PowerPoint Presentation**.
d. In the **Hyperlink to Other PowerPoint Presentation** dialog box, *click* the second presentation, and then *click* **OK**. The **Hyperlink to Slide** dialog box appears.
e. In the **Hyperlink to Slide** dialog box, under **Slide title**, *click* the slide that you want to link to, and then *click* **OK**.
f. *Click* **OK** in the **Action Settings** dialog box.

2. Create a link from the second presentation back to the first presentation:
    a. In the second presentation, select the text or object that you want to *click* to link to the first presentation.
    b. On the **Insert** tab, in the **Links** group, *click* **Action**.
    c. In the **Action Settings** dialog box, on either the **Mouse Click** tab or **Mouse Over** tab, *click* **Hyperlink To**, and then *click* **Other PowerPoint Presentation**.
    d. In the **Hyperlink to Other PowerPoint Presentation** dialog box, *click* the first presentation, and then *click* **OK**. The **Hyperlink to Slide** dialog box appears.

e. In the **Hyperlink to Slide** dialog box, under **Slide title**, *click* the slide that you want to link to, and then *click* **OK**.

f. *Click* **OK** in the **Action Settings** dialog box.

Changing Slide Order

When you create a presentation, you may want to change the order of your slides.

1 In the pane that contains the **Outline** and **Slides** tabs, *click* the **Slides** tab.

2 On the **Slides** tab, select the slide thumbnails that you want to move, and then *drag* them to their new location. To select multiple sequential slides, *click* the first slide, and then *hold CTRL* while you *click* the other slides that you want.

Or you can change the order of your slides by doing the following:

1 *Click* the **View** tab.

2 *Click* **Slide Sorter** in the **Presentation Views** group.

3 *Click and drag* the slide you want to move.

4 When you see a black horizontal line between the two slides that you want to place the selected slide, release the mouse.

Copy & Paste Slides

When you copy one or more slides from a presentation, and then paste them to a location either within the same presentation or to another presentation, you can specify the theme that you want the new slides to adopt.

When you paste a slide, it inherits the theme of the slide that precedes it. However, if you copy the slide from another presentation that uses a different theme, you can retain that theme when you paste the slide into a different presentation.

1 On the **View** tab, in the **Presentation Views** group, *click* **Normal.**
2 In the pane that contains the **Outline** and **Slides** tabs, *click* the **Slides** tab.
3 Select the slide that you want to copy by doing one of the following:

- To select a single slide, *click* it.
- To select multiple sequential slides, *click* the first slide, press *SHIFT*, and then *click* the last slide that you want.
- To select multiple non-sequential slides, press *CTRL*, and then *click* each slide that you want.

4 *Right-click* one of the selected slides, and then *click* **Copy**.
5 In the presentation into which you want to paste the copied slides, in the pane that contains the Outline and Slides tabs, on the **Slides** tab, *right-click* the slide that you want your copied slides to follow.
6 On the menu that appears when you *right-click*, under **Paste Options**, *click* on one of the following:

- **Destination Theme** - If you want the slide to take the theme of the destination presentation that you are pasting to.
- **Keep Source Formatting** - If you want the slide to maintain the theme of presentation that you are copying from.

In the pane that contains the **Outline** and **Slides** tabs, *click* the **Slides** tab, and then *right-click* the slide that you want your copied slides to follow.

To insert the slides between two existing slides**,** in the pane that contains the **Outline** and **Slides** tabs, *click* the **Slides** tab, and then *right-click* the slide that you want your copied slides to follow. You will see a black vertical flashing line. *Right-click* and *click* **Paste**. You can also *click* on the **Home** tab, in the **Clipboard** group, *click* **Paste**.

Change the Order of Stacked Objects

You can stack items such as objects, placeholders, or shapes (and even grouped objects) so that one appears in front of another. You can change the order in which each appears on a slide.

1 *Right-click* the object (or set of grouped objects) that you want to bring to the front or send to the back.

2 Do one of the following:

- To bring a slide object to the front of a group of stacked slide objects, point to **Bring to Front**, and then *click* **Bring to Front**.
- To move a slide object up one placement to the front in the stacking order, point to **Bring to Front**, and then *click* **Bring Forward**.

- To send a slide object to the back of a group of stacked slide objects, point to **Send to Back**, and then *click* **Send to Back**.
- To send a slide object one placement to the back in the stacking order, point to **Send to Back**, and then *click* **Send Backward**.

Or you can use the ribbon command.

1 *Click* on the object you want to move (can be a shape, picture, chart or video)

2 Go to the special tools tab (could be **Drawing Tools**, **Chart Tools**, or a **SmartArt Tools** special tools tab)

3 Under **Format** tab in the **Arrange** group, there is a **Bring Forward** and a **Send Backward** drop down button.

- In the **Bring Forward** drop down list are the options to **Bring Forward** or to **Bring to Front.**
- In the **Send Backward** drop down list are the options to **Send Backward** or to **Send to Back**.

Chapter 22 Giving the Presentation

Overview of animation and transitions

When it comes to animations and transitions, many times less is best. It is best to use no more than two different types of transitions between the slides. Too much animation takes the attention away from the presenter or the information and distracts the audience. Animation should aid in highlighting an important point in the presentation. Many times an exit animation is not needed unless you want to remove information to highlight the next part of the slide.

Highlight and Pin

To use a pin or highlight an item on your presentation while presenting your presentation in slide show, *right-click* the mouse and either *click* on **Pin** or **Highlight**.

Pausing during your presentation

If you need to pause during a presentation or you want to have the audience's full attention you might want to hide the slide and have the slide turn to a blank screen or a white screen. If you have not planned for the pause and not included a blank screen in the presentation you might find it helpful to either make the screen white or black while you pause.

To make the screen black during the presentation hit the **B** key. To get back to your presentation hit the **B** key again.

To make the screen white, hit the **W** key. To restart you presentation hit the **W** Key again.

Start your Presentation

After you have reviewed your presentation for spelling errors, slide order, color and objects with meaning and the other limitless items that you should do before the presentation, it is now time to test the slide show with all its transitions, animations and links.

1 *Click* on the **Slide Show** tab.
2 Under the **Start Slide Show** group *click* **From Beginning.**
3 The slide show starts. *Click* on the slide to advance to the next slide.
4 When an object has a link embedding on it, move the mouse over the object and *click* on the object. If you cannot find the link hit the **Tab** key and a frame will show around the first link.
5 When you are done with the linked file, either minimize or close the file. PowerPoint will open to the slide page with the link. *Click* the page (no on the object) to move to the next page.
6 When done, either continue to *click* the mouse or use the ***Esc*** key to exit the presentation.

To move forward in a presentation you can use one of the following methods:

1 *Left-click* the mouse.
2 Hit (slightly touch) the right arrow key.
3 Hit the down arrow key.
4 Hit the space bar.
5 Hit the Page down key.

To move back to the previous page or animation you can use one of the following methods:

1 Hit (slightly touch) the Backspace key.
2 Hit the up arrow key.

3 Hit the left arrow key.

4 Hit the Page up key.

To move to a particular slide during a slide show, enter the number of the slide that you want to go to and then hit **Enter**.

Hide or show a slide

If your presentation contains slides that provide different levels of detail, perhaps for different audiences, you can hide these slides so that they are not displayed in your main presentation. But you can still access them if you need to. When you hide a slide, the slide remains in the file even though it is hidden when you run the presentation in Slide Show view. You can switch the **Hide Slide** option on and off individually for any slide in the presentation.

1. In the **Slide/Outline** pane that contains the Outline and Slides tabs, *click* the **Slides** tab.

   To hide a slide, *right-click* the slide that you want to hide, and then *click* **Hide Slide**.
2. In the slide thumbnail on the **Slides** tab, the hidden slide has the slide number crossed out.
3. To re-show a hidden slide, *right-click* the slide, and then *click* **Hide Slide**.

If you are in Slide Show view and you decide that you want to show a slide that you previously hid, *right-click* the current slide, point to **Go to Slide**, and then *click* the slide that you want to show.

How to mark on your Presentation while in slide show

While you are in slide show and delivering your presentation you can draw on a slide. Follow these steps:

1. *Right-click* your mouse on the slide that you would like to mark on or draw on.
2. Select **Pointer Options**.
3. *Click* on **Pen**.
4. *Click and drag* as if you are writing.
5. When the slide show is done you will get a message window stating: "**Do you want to keep your ink annotations?**"
6. Mostly you will want to push the **Discard** button. Unless you did a great job of marking up your presentation then you might want to keep your art work.
7. If you want to erase the marks while giving your presentation use the *Ctrl+E* key, the **Eraser** will replace the **Pen** and you now can erase the marks. Or you can *right-click* during the slide show and select **Pointer Options**, then *click* on **Eraser**. Then move the eraser cursor to the markings and *click* on them.

Index

Made in United States
Orlando, FL
04 November 2026

90206048R00144